# THE HOUSE AT SHELBURNE FARMS

# THE HOUSE AT SHELBURNE FARMS

## THE STORY OF ONE OF AMERICA'S GREAT COUNTRY ESTATES

by Joe Sherman

Paul S. Eriksson, *Publisher*
Middlebury, Vermont

This book is for Maggie
and Andrew

© Copyright 1986, 1992 by Joe Sherman.

All rights reserved. No part of this work may be reproduced in any form by any means, electronic or mechanical, including photocopying and recording, or by any information storage or retrieval system, without permission in writing from Paul S. Eriksson, *Publisher,* Middlebury, Vermont 05753.

Grateful acknowledgement is made to Shelburne Farms Resources, from whose archives much of the material in the book was drawn. Other acknowledgements appear at the rear.

Manufactured in the United States of America

Revised Edition

10  9  8  7  6  5  4  3  2

**Library of Congress Cataloging-in-Publication Data**

Sherman, Joe, 1945-
    The house at Shelburne Farms : the story of one of America's great country estates / by Joe Sherman : introduction by Alec Webb. —
Rev. ed.
      p. cm.
    Includes bibliographical references.
    ISBN-0-8397-3353-4 : $19.95. — ISBN 0-8397-3352-6 (pbk.) : $12.95.
    1. Shelburne Farms (Vt.) 2. Vanderbilt family. 3. Webb family. 4. Vermont — Biography. I. Title.
F59.S49S49   1992
974.3'17 — dc20                                          92-14315
                                           CIP

Cover and book design by Eugenie S. Delaney.

# Introduction

Shelburne House has already seen several generations come and go. When I was born in 1952, my grandfather, Vanderbilt Webb, and father Derick Webb, were soliciting bids to have it demolished. The house had not been lived in year-round since the thirties. The furnace had been removed in the forties as scrap metal for the war effort. As it turned out, the bids came in higher than they could afford and the building was left for nature to dismantle.

At that time, my father's priority was developing an economically viable farm operation. There was no hope of ever being able to restore the architectural white elephants which he inherited in 1956. He built a dairy barn in the midst of his grandparents' and Olmsted's private "park" near Shelburne House and converted the old golf course into pasture. The Farm Barn and Coach Barn were used as temporary outbuildings for the dairy operation.

The Big House—which was the only name we ever knew it had—was not part of my early childhood experience. The home where my five brothers and sisters and I all grew up was almost a mile from the Big House but just a three-minute walk through the woods from the new dairy barn. This was our little world where we built forts, bicycled and played after school. Family history was hardly, if ever, discussed.

In the sixties, my parents decided to have a little fun by opening the Big House for the summer. Shutters were removed, water pipes turned on and we packed our bags to move into the few bedrooms that were still livable. We had a great time in our over-sized, falling-down camp and ended up enjoying a handful of teenage summers there. I remember days spent helping to rake and unload hay on the farm, swimming, running down long hallways, enjoying picnic dinners and playing late night games in the pool room. With the north wing unoccupied, we had no fear of disturbing adults sleeping at the other end of the house. Guests came and went, college students working on the farm stayed with us and one of the first large public events was held on the lawn—a gathering of American Field Service students. We grew to love the land and the beauty of Shelburne Farms. Without intending it, my parents had given the house and the farm new life and a new beginning.

By 1972 my brothers and sisters and I were deeply concerned about global issues threatening the future of the earth. We established a nonprofit corporation with the goal of using Shelburne Farms as a resource for environmental education—to teach and demonstrate the stewardship of natural and agricultural resources. A summer camp for children was started and our hope was that one day the whole farm could be used for a variety of public programs. My father eventually made this possible by giving the property to the nonprofit organization when he died in 1984.

After completing a long-range planning process, the board of trustees launched a three-phase Capital Campaign in 1985 to address the daunting task of expanding education programs, increasing opportunities for public access, restoring the historic buildings and landscape, and establishing a financially self-sustaining operation. Shelburne House was renovated as an inn to enable visitors to enjoy and learn about Shelburne Farms and to create a new source of revenue to help cover general operating and maintenance expenses.

Following models in Switzerland and England's Lake District, The Inn at Shelburne Farms links tourism with local agriculture, land conservation and historic preservation. In addition, each time guests stay or dine here, they provide funds needed to support our education and public programs.

1992, the 20th anniversary of Shelburne Farms Resources, Inc., marked the opening of our new archives at Shelburne House in honor of family archivist J. Watson Webb, Jr. Thanks to Watson's inspiration and documentation and preservation of the history of Shelburne Farms, the heritage of Shelburne Farms is properly acknowledged for the continuity and meaning it gives to the future.

The incredible vision, generosity, commitment, and expertise of trustees, contributors, volunteers and staff has turned an impossible dream into a significant environmental education organization and a valuable community resource. The Inn at Shelburne Farms—Shelburne House—has played and continues to play a leading role in this transformation. Another chapter has been added to what, I hope you will agree, is an interesting story. It is ironic that the revitalization of the property to serve a future-oriented mission has also given us a new appreciation of its past.

ALEC WEBB
President

# Contents

There's no use trying, she said.
One *can't* believe impossible things.

I daresay you haven't had much practice,
said the Queen. When I was your age, I
always did it for half-an-hour a day.
Why, sometimes I've believed as many as
six impossible things before breakfast.

Lewis Carroll, *Alice in Wonderland*

# Beginnings

*Dr. William Seward Webb*

A stranger in a buckboard appeared at Edward Saxton's door in 1885 and offered to buy his farm overlooking Lake Champlain. The farmer gave him an option and later sold. One of the largest houses in Vermont soon squatted in Saxton's apple orchard, only to be displaced within a decade by the biggest house in the state, a Y-shaped mansion of a hundred rooms manned by thirty servants and overseeing a four thousand acre agricultural estate.

The owner of the house and the estate was Dr. W. Seward Webb, president of the Wagner Palace Car Company, a Vanderbilt railroad enterprise.

Dr. Webb had first traveled to Vermont five years earlier, in 1880, scouting out the Rutland Railroad as a possible Vanderbilt takeover. Although his report to his boss, William Henry Vanderbilt, was negative on the railroad, his enthusiasm for Vermont was unconstrained. Engaged to marry Vanderbilt's daughter, Lila, the young man immediately took his fiancée north where she found the Burlington area as captivating as he had.

They married in 1881, returned, rented a house, and began work on Oakledge, a rambling, gabled house with lots of porches and a lawn sloping down towards the lake.

A move this far north for people of their social circles was quite radical for Victorian times. This was the era of country estates, and Oakledge provided them with one of modest size, but most such retreats from the ills of urbanization clustered around established pleasure centers, namely Newport, Saratoga Springs, and, for the adventurous, Bar Harbor, downeast in Maine.

But Burlington, Vermont?

Speculations are varied and debatable as to why the young married couple, with an infant daughter and another child on the way, established their country place this far north. Evidently, the doctor-turned-businessman was smitten first by the physical beauty. Burlington sat on a slope overlooking one of the most gorgeous bodies of water in the United States. On the far shore sprawled the high peaks of the Adirondacks, an alluring, purplish wilderness in the summer twilight. To the east were the Green Mountains, Mount Mansfield dominating that jagged spine. Burlington itself possessed a youthful vitality. Men of means were exploring their business potential there, sending timber and other goods south via rail and water. Architectural gems were being built in large number. And in one of these gems, overlooking the lake and Shelburne Point to the south, lived Colonel LeGran Cannon.

On a sizeable local scale, if small by New York City standards, Colonel Cannon had created an estate of his own. He had his large home overlooking the city and the lake, and a breeding farm in Shelburne. He managed a Lake George steamship line and owned other businesses. Like Dr. Webb, he had deep military roots and obviously preferred this wilder north country to the more civilized terrain to the south. Whether the men became close friends is not known, but the elder Cannon seems to have become, to some extent, a role model for the ambitious railroad president from New York.

It is not unlikely that while visiting the colonel, Dr. Webb looked slightly south of his own modest Oakledge and coveted a stunning hook of land that jutted out into the water: Shelburne Point.

He had an interesting proprietary connec-

*Lawn tennis at Oakledge, ca. 1884. Located in Burlington on Lake Champlain, Oakledge was a relatively modest country estate for a young Victorian couple as wealthy and well connected as Lila and Dr. Webb.*

tion to property adjoining this point. His grandfather, General Samuel B. Webb, who had fought with distinction in the Revolutionary War, had been granted the Lone Tree Hill area, not two miles south, for his years of military service. Later he had sold the land. But it is easy to imagine a sense of predestination here.

Other reasons the Webbs settled in Burlington may have included a dream Dr.

Webb had, a dream shared by most railroad men of the time, of building his own "road," something he did accomplish within a decade with the construction of the Mohawk and Malone Railroad through the Adirondacks. He may also have harbored ambition to become governor of Vermont, and at the turn of the century he would make a run for the Republican nomination.

And although women in Victorian times

*The Webb family on a porch at Oakledge, ca. 1886*

were conditioned to support, unquestioning, their husbands, it could not have hurt that Lila liked Burlington and the area, too.

As for the cold Vermont winters, the Webbs returned to their Fifth Avenue mansion for the first few years. Yet they had a certain fondness for the snow, attested to by an article in the *Burlington Free Press,* February 20, 1885. The Webbs and their guests had arrived in town the previous night aboard a private car, and on Sunday morning proceeded to do some coasting down Main Street. Horses hauled their sleigh up the long rolled hill, and:

Arriving at the top of the hill, the team was sent back to warn unwary foot passengers and other teams of the near approach of the coasters, and when all was in readiness, away the party sped down Main Street, shooting by the trees and other objects at railroad speed and leaving behind them a cloud of snow.

A large crowd gathered to rate the New Yorkers' coasting abilities. Judging by the tongue-in-cheek conclusion of the article, evidently, in those days, for a gentleman estate owner, an apology to the mayor was sufficient defense for having broken a city

regulation. Coasting on city streets was against the law.

That summer, with an uncanny sense of impending resources, Dr. Webb began to buy property along the lake shore in Shelburne. These resources came his way in December when William Henry Vanderbilt, age sixty-five, died of apoplexy in his Fifth Avenue mansion. Vanderbilt's worth exceeded $200 million. Lila inherited a relatively small share of that, some $10 million, and her house on Vanderbilt row in New York. Some idea of how much money $10 million was is suggested by the fact that the government of the State of New York, then by far the most populous state in the nation, operated for a year on a little less.

With this sudden influx of money Dr. Webb had the resources to shape his life in the Burlington area just about any way he saw fit. There would be frequent business trips between New York and his new home, but for those he had the luxury coaches of his own Wagner Palace Car Company at his disposal. His travels to Brazil as a boy, then to Europe as a medical student, and later around the Eastern United States on business, had shown his penchant for the click of the rails. Dr. Webb was then, and would be until confined to a wheelchair late in life, a man who loved to travel, who loved to ride the rails.

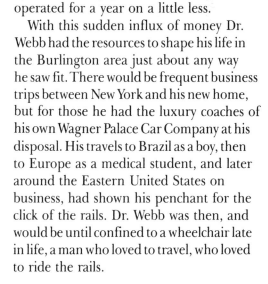

# The Webbs and the Vanderbilts

*Dr. Webb and James Watson, ca. 1888*

W. Seward Webb's earliest known ancestors lived for over two hundred years near Stratford-on-Avon where their bloodline entangled with William Shakespeare's. Four brothers of one Alexander Webb left England and sailed to America during the early 1600s. From one of these brothers, Richard, W. Seward Webb was descended through a line dominated by soldiers.

His father, James Watson Webb, was a fiery, independent young man who ran away from home at age seventeen, made his way to Washington, and enlisted in the army. He rose to the rank of general fighting the Winnebago Indians just west of frontier Chicago in the 1820s, then retired from the military at the age of twenty-seven to return to New York and become the owner and editor of the New York *Courier and Enquirer*. In that position he remained reckless, getting into political entanglements and duels, and acquired a reputation as a competitive, enterprising and outspoken businessman.

W. Seward Webb's grandfather, General Samuel B. Webb, fought at Bunker Hill at age nineteen. A journal writer extraordinaire, he recorded that famous fight and others in a colorful, expressive hand. Captured by the British on Long Island, then freed in an exchange of prisoners, he went on to serve as one of Washington's aides-de-camp. After the Revolutionary War he held the Bible on which President Washington took his first oath of office, and was deeded property in Shelburne, Vermont, as payment for his years of meritorious service.

A brother of W. Seward's, Alexander S. Webb, was also a general. This distinguished family member was wounded both at Gettysburg and at Spottsylvania, where a Confederate bullet grazed his temple.

W. Seward Webb's mother, Laura Virginia Cram, was the daughter of a New York merchant, Jacob Cram.

As a boy he was privately tutored. He went with his father to Brazil during the Civil War, where the flamboyant newspaperman was acting American ambassador. Later, as a young man, he was sent to military school to prepare him, no doubt, to some day join the ranks of Webb-family generals. Something deterred him from becoming a soldier though, and after attending Columbia University for two years, he elected to go into medicine. In 1875 he graduated from the College of Physicians and Surgeons of New York. He then went abroad to Vienna to continue his medical education for two more years.

Upon his return to New York, however, the medical profession, like the military, for some reason lost its appeal for him.

The era he found himself in, the so-called Gilded Age, was a time of great optimism. A future shaped by science and controlled by men promised boundless progress. Incredible fortunes, the likes of which had never been known in this country, were being amassed. Competitive battles for wealth and power were creating new industries and jobs, but were also polluting rivers, denuding vast tracts of virgin forest, and pulling thousands of people off the farms to jam the growing cities. In this whirl, expectations on all levels of society were rising. Those of the rich ascended into an airy region verging on dream. They were wealthy beyond their wildest expectations. Their lives became long-term pursuits of visions once thought the exclusive province of monarchs and kings.

Overseeing all this were businessmen.

Politics played handmaiden to their power. The yardstick for conduct and manners was English Victorian. And ironically, as more and more people abandoned the land for a small piece of this dream, the rich countered their momentum by pursuing a vision of a bygone American pastoral ideal whose elements were rooted in the pre-Civil War agrarian era of their grandfathers: the gentleman's country estate. All one needed was money. And for a young man disenchanted with his occupation, and with the right connections to move himself into the business mainstream, the promise of money and power and a country estate must have exercised an intoxicating allure.

For W. Seward Webb it did. In 1879 he left the rather moribund medical profession for the fast paced action of Wall Street.

Soon after, he went to work for William Henry Vanderbilt, the railroad magnate, for whom he first traveled to Vermont on business, and to whom he proved his business acumen by rescuing a floundering Wagner Palace Car Company from the economic doldrums. A year after that, in 1881, he married Vanderbilt's daughter, Lila.

## Lila Osgood Vanderbilt

In 1640 Jan Aertson van der Bilt (Jan Aertson, from the village of Bilt in Holland),

*Lila Webb, ca. 1883*

crossed the Atlantic, served three years as an indentured servant, and started a farm on Long Island. His descendants carved out farms in the wild and forested reaches of Staten Island, and supplied fresh produce for the growing borough of Manhattan. New Dorp, on Staten Island, remained the family seat, and it was there, in May, 1794, that Cornelius van Derbilt, future scion of the family, was born.

The young man grew up to change the spelling of the family name again and to make it infamous.

When not quite out of his teens, Cornelius Vanderbilt decided that he did not like sailing vegetables over to New York as well as his father and grandfather had. Combining a shrewd business sense with ruthless competitive tactics, he expanded Vanderbilt interests into steamboat transportation and the burgeoning railroad network uniting the growing cities. By the time of Lila Vanderbilt's birth in 1860, her grandfather, the commodore, was a legend. A large man, white haired and raw mannered, he had little tolerance for royal forebears or high society. To get his way, he bribed politicians. To expand his empire, he conspired against his transportation competition. He outlived his wife and threw his heirs into turmoil when, in his seventies, he proposed to a woman forty years his junior, and she ac-

cepted. Admired, hated, but always respected, the commodore was by 1870 the richest man in America.

William Henry Vanderbilt, his eldest son and Lila's father, was not held in very high esteem by the commodore. In fact, suffering from poor health and insufficient business aggressiveness, William Henry had been exiled to the family farm in New Dorp. Interestingly enough, it was there, on Staten Island, where William Henry made the acquaintance of another exile: Frederick Law Olmsted. The father-to-be of American landscape architecture, farming not because he wanted to but because he hadn't yet found what he wanted to do, shared his thoughts on agricultural improvements with Vanderbilt in 1848. This fortuitous relationship eventually had long-term effects on the design of thousands of acres of parks and estates, one of which became Shelburne Farms.

It also seems significant to note that Lila Vanderbilt spent some of her youth on a farm on Staten Island. There she may have grown fond of flowers, carrying this influence with her to the Shelburne Farms house and gardens decades ahead. Privileged and protected as she undoubtedly was, Lila must have smelled and heard and seen the crops being harvested. And may have stood on the windy shore and

watched the boats laden with Staten Island vegetables ply the waters of what is now called the Verrazano Narrows, heading for the crowded docks of a thriving Manhattan.

When William Henry Vanderbilt improved his health and exhibited some shrewd business sense managing the family farming interests, he was returned to New York by the commodore to assume day-to-day operations of the Hudson River Railroad, and then the New York Central.

Manhattan became the family's business headquarters and pleasure playground. They were elite members of a new American gentry. They were expected to own yachts and horses and private rail cars. They were expected to travel abroad annually, to overindulge their appetites and senses. To be wealthy and frugal was to be eccentric. William Henry Vanderbilt, growing accustomed to the style associated with wealth and power, built a fifty-eight room mansion on Fifth Avenue, employing six hundred men for a year and a half.

It was in this atmosphere that Lila came of age. She attended Miss Porter's School in Connecticut, studying the things a young lady in high society was supposed to know: French, art appreciation, manners. She kept journals and wrote plays, one of which still survives, "Faithfulness Rewarded: A Tale of Maggie Martin." Like her peers, Lila was

*In March, 1883, the Vanderbilts put on a lavish costume ball in New York. Lila, shown here, went dressed as a hornet.*

being groomed for marriage. An ambitious man would do, hopefully of means, and definitely with character. If that man already happened to be working for her father, that was not to be held against him.

Once Lila married W. Seward Webb in 1881, they lived most of the year in a mansion on Fifth Avenue, which had become almost a Vanderbilt block, and traveled north by private train to Burlington for the summer. Their life together was one of privilege, status and entertainment.

For instance, a costume ball put on by Lila's sister-in-law in March, 1883, became known as the most flamboyant party ever thrown in New York. Men dressed as knights, as sailors, as figures from popular paintings. Women costumed themselves as Mother Goose figures and duchesses. Lila came dressed as a hornet. Groups of eight danced rehearsed quadrilles from George Washington's time. Ex-president Ulysses S. Grant was there. The following day the papers claimed more than $75 thousand had been spent. The occasion was compared to Versailles. The Vanderbilts had just put on the most lavish ball in America.

That same year Dr. Webb was elected president of the Wagner Palace Car Company, a Vanderbilt enterprise. The following year, in 1882, construction began on his modest country estate, Oakledge, in Burlington, Vermont.

*Thirty-plus farms eventually comprised the estate. This map shows purchases made between 1885 and 1891. Saxton's Point is on the left, a bluff once part of Edward Saxton's 72.55 acres.*

# Shelburne Farms: An Agricultural Estate

By June, 1886, Dr. Webb was well on his way to acquiring the thirty small farms that included his grandfather's post-Revolutionary War holdings on Lone Tree Hill and the Edward Saxton Farm. To advise him on a plan to knit all these farms together in a visually harmonious whole, the doctor retained the services of Frederick Law Olmsted, the landscape architect whose Natural Style was favored by estate builders of the Victorian era.

Olmsted toured the lake front, the orchards and woodlots, the meadows and pastures that had been acquired, and proposed that Dr. Webb create a park-like setting alongside Lake Champlain with his house overlooking the water.

The site of the house in this park seems to have remained in doubt for some time. J.P. Cotton, who surveyed the land in the fall of 1886, referred to Saxton's Point as the favored spot, although Arthur Taylor, manager of the accumulated acreage, told him that was not definite. Cotton passed this information along to Olmsted by letter in September, and advised him that additional farms were being bought as he worked, complicating the surveying job.

As might have been expected, not all the farmers were eager to sell. Dr. Webb had gotten options on practically all their farms by sending his agent around during the week. When the farmers had learned that they had all given options to the same stranger in a buckboard, they were irate. Some now were reluctant to go through with a sale, so boundaries were tenuous during this acquisition stage. In fact, in a letter written early in 1886, manager Taylor urged Dr. Webb to act promptly on the options, and mentioned one woman farmer who refused to name a price. Most were easier to negotiate with, however; Taylor claimed thirteen farms had been optioned, including, "...all the Beautiful high lands in that whole district."

What was most obvious, despite changing boundaries and prospective house sites, was the size and scope of the emerging estate. The fact that Frederick Law Olmsted, the

*Hopes ran high that the Farms would set new standards in agriculture and pass them along to small farmers. Pictured here is a McCormick reaper, a machine for cutting standing grain.*

heralded landscape visionary (environmentalist had not yet entered the American vocabulary), was advising Dr. Webb on the overall design lent considerable prestige to the project.

## Frederick Law Olmsted's Natural Style

Olmsted's genius had by this time significantly altered the way Americans looked at their landscape. His reputation was rooted in his design, in partnership with Calvert Vaux, of Central Park in New York City, undertaken in the late 1850s. Olmsted went on to design numerous urban parks, including Mount Royal in Montreal, Jackson Park in Chicago, and the Boston Park System, as well as many college campuses, before turning to estates in the Gilded Age. Tanglewood, in Lenox, Massachusetts, became his first estate design in 1883.

All these precedent-setting projects were guided by a simple yet profound principle that was far ahead of its time: an exposure to nature was fundamental for man's physical and spiritual wellbeing.

Frederick Law Olmsted had been born when America was a nation of farmers and had seen the country evolve into an industrialized world power. Whereas most men embraced this progress, Olmsted examined

*Frederick Law Olmsted designed a sensuous, park-like landscape. Here, tall elms shade a curving lakeside drive.*

it. He saw progress not only improving people's living conditions but gathering them tightly together in the cities as well. He saw it marring land and depleting resources. He worked not so much to halt this change, but to set aside certain pristine places where nature offered contrast, and a respite. These urban parks he constructed provided much needed psychological balm for the human spirit. When gentlemen's estates became the vogue, he applied the innovative methods he had developed over four decades in the cities to large tracts of land in the country.

Thus, when the elderly Olmsted rode a carriage around Dr. Webb's acquired farms in 1886, he was famous, and deservedly so.

His specific recommendations came to Dr. Webb by letter in July, 1887. An accompanying sketch suggested distinct farm, park and forest divisions, all connected by roads. Curiously enough, the proposed location for the house had changed again. It was no longer on Saxton's Point, but centered in the landscape on top of Lone Tree Hill, elevation five hundred and fifteen feet, a half mile away from the lake and about three hundred feet above it, perched on what had been General Samuel B. Webb's property a century before. This new location commanded views of forest, farms and gardens. A large park separated the residence from Quaker Smith Point which curved out into Lake Champlain.

These recommendations from Olmsted, although not carried out exactly, were adhered to in principle. Under Dr. Webb's direction, and manager Arthur Taylor's supervision, an estate that exemplified the planner's Natural Style slowly emerged.

Shelburne Farms became park-like yet eclectic, planted with indigenous vegetation to blend the altered landscape with the undisturbed one surrounding it. Miles of macadamed roads (in 1888 a stone-crushing machine was bought for the purpose of grinding red granite for their surfacing) followed the natural contours of the land. Tall trees along these roads dappled them with shade in the summer. There were forest lanes, rolling meadows and lakeside vistas. The farm areas alternated with the woodlands and the pleasure grounds of the house. Many visitors noted the long carriage ride from Shelburne Station to the house, a macadamed drive of several miles beneath spreading elms.

This natural order given shape created a pastoral painting in which man played the role of the artist. It was an irony of the age:

*Miles of macadamed roads connected all parts of the estate: home grounds, forests (as pictured here), and Farms.*

men whose wealth came from the dynamics of change and impact desired retreats reminiscent of their pre-industrial past, of the land of their grandfathers.

Shelburne Farms belonged to this estate vision yet went beyond it.

As an almost sensuous landscape, one which emphasized the natural and tried to create a very satisfying painting, Shelburne Farms exemplified the country estate ideal of the times. But as a large working farm, one where hopes ran high that experimentation and breeding would set new standards, it moved beyond the conventional. Central to the vision from its inception was this farm of the new age, vast in dimension, functioning outside typical economic restraints, embracing both the pastoral landscape of yesterday and the scientific farm of tomorrow. A not-so-distant visual past surrounded and defined a desirable agricultural future. This concept of an experimental farm in an inspired landscape distinguished Shelburne Farms from all the others.

To achieve his goal, Dr. Webb also used the limited services of Gifford Pinchot, another visionary who brought to forest conservation what his colleague and friend, Frederick Law Olmsted, had brought to landscape architecture: a visionary's conviction of its importance. Pinchot recognized

that short-term uses of land and resources often defiled both. A pivotal figure in the growing American Conservation Movement, he was not opposed to development, but was opposed to wastefulness, mismanagement and shortsightedness, and spent much of his life crusading for an expanded environmental awareness.

Burlington may have struck Pinchot as a small city where hard conservation choices had been made with the usual adverse effects. Most of the local timber had been over-cut decades before. Now hundreds of barges plied the lake, hauling logs down from Canada and across from the Adirondacks. Lakeside Burlington presented a teeming zone of industry where factories clustered side-by-side for over a mile and a half. The factories sawed and planed the logs into lumber. Doors, sills, furniture, barrels, boxes and dozens of other wooden products were manufactured and, along with building materials, shipped south to Boston and New York via the railroad. The conflict between utility and beauty along the Burlington lakeshore had been won by the former.

The extent of Pinchot's contributions to the Farms is unclear, as no written documentation survives. But his conservation philosophy, which focused on long-term stewardship rather than immediate exploita-

tion, obviously made a lasting impression on Dr. Webb when the young forester visited. Pinchot did direct some plantings of trees on the estate, and subsequently surveyed the timber on Dr. Webb's Nehasane, a game park of forty thousand acres in the Adirondacks.

Along with Olmsted, Pinchot moved down to North Carolina in the late 1880s, where he worked on a forestry management plan for Biltmore, the one hundred thousand acre estate being created by Lila's younger brother, George Vanderbilt.

## A Passion for Horses

A passion for horses also had a strong effect on the shape of Shelburne Farms. Just how strong an effect is suggested by a letter Dr. Webb, as a young man, received from his father, warning him to refrain from raising horses. Their breeding was a risky business demanding greater means than he was likely to acquire, James Watson Webb advised his son.

Once those means were firmly in hand, Dr. Webb set up a breeding operation of tremendous size and ambition. The barn was the largest in America, stabling over three hundred animals. Dr. Webb was convinced that Vermonters had crossbred too many trotters and mares, saddling farmers

*Inside the Breeding Barn, a groom holds the reins of a hackney, the all-purpose horse Dr. Webb had great expectations for. The barn, which had stables for three hundred animals, was large enough for games of indoor polo to be played.*

with a skinny horse that could carry them quickly to the station but hardly pull a plow. He intended to change this situation by breeding a refined all-purpose hackney, a strong, stocky horse that could both pull the plow and take the farmer to town in style. His goal, ironically, blinded him to the fact that the internal-combustion engine was in the process of making just such a horse as obsolete as the carriages it pulled.

Yet, during the formative years of Shelburne Farms, the importance of the horse continued unchallenged. Everyone, from the smallest lad to the oldest spinster, was familiar with trotters, roadsters, hackneys, four-in-hands and broughams, those elegant four-wheeled enclosed carriages with the driver perched out front. Practically everything, once you were away from the railroad tracks, went by horsepower not yet enclosed by steel.

*The* Ellesmere, *Dr. Webb's private rail car, somewhere in the American West in the late 1880s. The doctor (center left, seated on rail) traveled often with his family or with hunting companions.*

## Luxury on Rails

When Dr. Webb wanted to move enclosed by steel, he boarded the *Ellesmere*, his private rail car built by the Wagner Palace Car Company, of which he had become the president. From New York City to Shelburne, Vermont, required but one night's travel. This relative ease of transportation between the hub of the railroad business and his country estate allowed the doctor to reside legally in Vermont and still get quickly to New York when the need arose. The *Ellesmere*, attached to a locomotive, a baggage car, a dining car, and the *Marquita*, an older private car, also allowed the Webbs to travel practically anywhere they wanted in North America.

Taking advantage of this opportunity, in March, 1889, the Webbs, their three children, and some relatives and close friends traveled eighteen thousand miles in what the press called the ultimate blend of sport and pleasure.

Four cars and a locomotive made up the train, and a staff of fifteen servants, porters, cooks and waiters made it function. On route, they zigzagged across the American

*A five-storied structure with an enclosed courtyard of two acres, the Farm Barn housed shops for blacksmiths, carpenters, painters and managerial staff, as well as stalls for eighty teams of mules and horses.*

West and ended up in Vancouver, from where they steamed by ship up to Alaska. Frequently, the men removed shotguns, rifles and fishing gear from the baggage car to exercise their skills. The women and children watched and listened from the *Marquita,* second in the line of four cars. Three nurses accompanied Lila to take care of Frederica, James Watson and Seward, Jr. Three salons, a bath, a children's playroom with a large glass window, and a kitchen made up the *Marquita's* interior.

A dining car with seating for thirty separated the women from the men. The men traveled in the *Ellesmere.* Furnished and decorated in the eclectic, heavy, ornate style associated with masculinity, the *Ellesmere* had a piano for entertainment and an observation room at the rear with a window as wide as the car for watching the countryside recede in the distance.

The Webbs returned to Shelburne Farms for the summer.

Just a few facts from this busy period suggest the size and scope of the estate they returned to:

The Farm Barn, a five-storied stone and timber structure with two wings enclosing a two acre courtyard, had shops for blacksmiths, carpenters, painters and management staff, as well as stalls for eighty teams of mules and horses.

In 1890 the Farms ledger listed, among others, the following projects: the planting of two thousand seven hundred and sixty-five new trees, the transplanting of one thousand two hundred and ninety-four other trees, the harvesting of oats, wheat and rye, the sale of butter, milk, eggs and apples in New York, the building of new fences, the drilling of a gas well and the erection of telephone lines, the construction of new macadam roads using stone from the crusher in the quarry, the finishing of the Farm Barn wings, additional building of greenhouses, sheep and poultry and dairy buildings, and the completion of the Breeding Barn and the water works.

At any one time, several hundred employees were usually working.

# Building the House

*A temporary Shingle Style cottage designed by architect R.H. Robertson was built in 1887-1888 at a cost of about $30 thousand. This view was of the South Porch.*

The tale of the construction of the house began with the March, 1887 issue of "American Architect and Building News." In the magazine, Dr. Webb's friend and architect, Robert H. Robertson, published a rendering and floor plan of the place. They show a sprawling stone manor with a massive central unit, rear wings, and a curved arm, or loggia, terminated by a round tower in which a school room occupies the floor above the billiard room. In front there are two porches and a terrace with a fountain. Inside there are dozens of rooms. The whole thing suggests a railroad station for a medium-sized city.

The Webbs, after seeing the plans, evidently restrained Robertson. For in the fall of that year ground was broken on Saxton's Point and construction began on a cottage, as the Victorians quaintly called their summer homes. The cottage was meant to be temporary. In a few years the main residence would go up on Lone Tree Hill. Robertson must have been placated; he drew several additional renderings for the doctor to consider, including one of a huge Greek Revival mansion and another of an equally large stone castle.

Seeing the rejected renderings, and the large number of proposed designs the architect submitted, it is apparent that working for Dr. Webb was not easy. The man was constantly traveling, had railroad companies to worry about, as well as this country estate, and had just come into an immense fortune it must have taken a little time to get used to. The options he now could consider must have at times perplexed him. As for country-home architecture, precedents did exist, yet many were extravagant variations of an already dated style: French Renaissance. Dr. Webb seems to have wanted a house more symbolic of who he was and where he had decided to live. To add to the complexity, architecture itself was going through difficult growing pains.

With this in mind, the fact that a Shingle Style cottage was built in 1887-88 suggests the doctor was tempted to break with the grander styles of his in-laws and friends in Newport, Saratoga Springs and Bar Harbor. The Shingle Style was peculiarly American and utilized a low-cost material abundantly available: shingles. For this era it seemed almost a symbolic gesture downward, toward everyman.

*Clean of line and harmonious with its surroundings, the cottage had a sense of imposing charm. This view was from the east, as one approached by carriage.*

## The Shingle Style Cottage

The cottage Robertson designed was countryish, two stories high, with tall, thin windows, a shingled roof and second story, and clapboards (this complementary, inexpensive material appeared occasionally in Shingle Style houses) closer to the ground. Squatty in appearance, it was a hundred twenty-eight feet long and fifty feet wide. A porte-cochère sheltered part of the drive turnaround. A circular, conical-roofed porch faced south. Tall chimneys, a bulging half tower, and minimal decorative touches, kept the cottage clean of line and harmonious with its surroundings. Overall, it had a sense of imposing charm.

Inside the entrance, on the right, were Dr. Webb's office and a gun room. According to surviving blueprints, the dining room, breakfast room, library, drawing room, kitchen and larders also occupied the ground floor. Upstairs, off an open hall, were the bedrooms, dressing rooms.

boudoir and two large nurseries facing the lake. A smaller day nursery, the nurse's room, the housekeeper's room, guest bedrooms and various closets and linen rooms completed the second floor. Four servants' rooms were on the small third floor.

Some idea of the scope of the construction of this cottage is suggested by the fact that twenty-five carpenters were laid off when the interior plastering was finished. It had to dry before additional interior work could be started.

Dr. Webb, Lila and their three small children, James Watson, Frederica and W. Seward, Jr., lived here while the agricultural estate took on new dimensions. A fourth child, Vanderbilt Webb, was born in 1891.

By late 1892 more than three thousand acres had been amassed. Lake frontage extended for over six miles with terrain changing from sandy beach to high cliffs overlooking the water. Fifteen miles of macadamed roads, surfaced with red granite, allowed travel to all corners of the estate. By then the places a guest might visit via horseback or carriage were many.

The huge Breeding Barn, center of its own complex and big enough for games of polo to be played inside, had just been completed. It housed stallions and mares and the stock Dr. Webb hoped would sire his rejuvenated hackney for all-

*The Webbs on the South Porch, ca. 1899. From left to right, Mrs. H. Walter Webb, Van, James Watson, Lila, Seward, Jr., H. Walter Webb and Dr. Webb.*

purpose farm use.

The five-storied Farm Barn stood two miles from the house. A visitor in June might have seen large numbers of laborers handling the ricks of hay needed to feed the mules through the winter. Out in the meadows teamsters worked these mules, tongues clicking, sharp blades cutting down the grass.

There were three acres of greenhouses to

visit, where all kinds of flowers, palms and vegetables were cultivated. Or one could peer into pens at furry ewes on the sheep and poultry farm.

A technological marvel, a reservoir, had just been finished up on Lone Tree Hill. There, a vista of the estate and the Green Mountains and Lake Champlain spread three hundred and sixty degrees all around. This reservoir was a hundred feet long, twenty feet wide and ten feet deep. Twelve thousand gallons of water could be drawn up from the lake in an hour, then piped via underground lines anywhere on the estate.

Exactly why the reservoir was built up there, instead of either the manor or the castle that Robertson had imagined, and the Webbs had considered, is not known. The site had proprietary appeal because of General Samuel Webb's ownership, offered a commanding view, and possessed a certain historical charm.

The story went that during the Battle of Plattsburg, in 1812, only one man was left in Shelburne. With the women and children, he had climbed the hill overlooking the shore where the boats had been outfitted with guns, and watched the decisive naval battle some eighteen miles across the lake.

As for the truth of the matter, it is possible that a castle or manor had become too expensive for the Webbs to build, either up on Lone Tree Hill or anywhere. Large sums of money were being poured into the buildings and operations of Shelburne Farms, and no profits were forthcoming. Simultaneously, Dr. Webb's major business, the Wagner Palace Car Company, was losing a legal battle to George Pullman, president of the Pullman Palace Car Company, for an infringement of patent. The ramifications of this business reversal led, eventually, to Pullman's gaining control of the Wagner Palace Car Company. The effect on the family finances must have been considerable.

It is also plausible that the Webbs, after living on Saxton's Point, gained respect for the lake winds and decided against any kind of house perched up so high. Or that Saxton's Point, with a physical enchantment all its own, enticed the family into reconsidering any move, alluring them into making what was temporary their year-round home.

Whatever the reason, or reasons, for the change of site and scale, as the estate grew, so did the need for a main residence. A temporary cottage did not suffice as the family headquarters of what was becoming "the" model agricultural estate in America.

## The Queen Anne Style

A design that eventually satisfied the Webbs aesthetically and economically was a house in the eclectic Queen Anne Style. The Shingle Style cottage, completely altered on the outside, but retaining some original interior design, became a starting point for the new and much larger residence.

Queen Anne at the time was the most popular domestic architectural style in America. It had little to do with Queen Anne, actually, or with the Renaissance style favored during her reign, from 1702 to 1714. Its popularity resulted from the influence of English architect, Richard Norman Shaw, and his followers. They had loosely adapted the medieval manor house of the late Middle Ages in England to the mid-1800s.

Those large, often fortified, manor houses of the Middle Ages were informal in layout. Form tended to follow function. The parapets were sometimes castellated so there was both a place from which to dump hot oil down onto invaders and another to duck behind when the arrows flew. Towers functioned as lookouts. Exposed timbers supported the frame.

Frustrated architects in the Victorian era, feeling stifled by the formal, classical design precedents they inherited, looked way back to these older and informal functional features, and reworked them. In the Stick Style they exposed the support beams and timbers, filling between with wattle-and-daub. In the Shingle Style, they clothed them all in a unifying element, shingles. In the Queen Anne Style, they articulated their separateness with various materials and elements to break up the surface the shingles tried to unite. H.H. Richardson, the most famous American practitioner of Victorian architecture, whose Richardson Romanesque was a unique blend of traditional sources, sculptured shapes and structural arches, all focused into a personal

*This Robertson blueprint of a side gable illustrates some of the architectural and decorative details of the eclectic Queen Anne Style, such as dentils (A), clustered chimneys (B), brackets (C), half-timbering (D), bay windows (E), a dormer (F), diamond-motif windows (G), stained glass (H), large, plain sash (I), and a cornice band (J).*

statement, managed to rise above the influences. But then he was a genius.

Dr. Webb's architect, Robert Robertson, worked freely in all the various Victorian styles. His reputation was based on train depots (he may have met Dr. Webb while designing depots for the Hudson Valley Railroad), churches and society cottages. In Dr. Webb, Robertson must have realized he had found a man with tastes as eclectic as his own. Their partnership lasted for many years, with Robertson being responsible for the design of all the major structures at Shelburne Farms. He also built one of New York's first skyscrapers, the twenty-seven-story Park Row Building, but history would point to his years of work at Shelburne Farms as the pinnacle of his career.

When it came time to act on the main residence, this eclectic camaraderie between the doctor and Robertson united with the dominant Queen Anne Style architecture to build the house that stands today.

## Specifications and Construction

In March, 1895, architect Robertson submitted specifications and blueprints for conversion of the cottage into a main residence roughly triple its size. The servants' wing was to be moved several hundred feet north and turned into an annex. The roof of the cottage was to be raised, a story added, and the manorial style emphasized with clustered chimneys, half-timbering (a system of construction which leaves support timbers exposed and fills between them), and stucco. A large new wing, called the Westerly Extension, was to be constructed. An attached smaller wing for the servants was to be built in back. The style throughout was to be freestyle Queen Anne. When completed, the house would contain over a hundred rooms, and would change shape from the long central block of the cottage to a compound-Y.

No photographs exist of the construction, although we do have Robertson's blueprints of floor plans, elevations and details such as the front of the large Mosler safe in the Silver Cleaning Room and a full-scale drawing of the fireplace mantel and surrounds in the Northwest Bedroom (now called the Colonial Room). His eighteen pages of specifications for the Westerly Extension are particularly enlightening regarding materials and methods of construction, which can be presumed to have been used throughout.

Local stone went into the foundation walls. All structural timber for floors, walls, partitions and the roof, was "well seasoned, good quality spruce, free from shakes, knots, sap, splits and other defects, square edged and of a uniform thickness."

Balloon-framing had recently revolutionized construction methods, allowing for varied and fancy shapes never even considered with post-and-beam frames, and it was used throughout. Large dimension lumber supported floors and the roof, but most wall and interior work was done with the standard two by four. Once completed, the frame was enclosed with spruce, and a layer of tarpaper went over everything before carpenters nailed down the finished exterior — clapboards for the first story and shingles for the second.

Shingles covered the roof as well, laid five inches to the weather. The Munson black slate roof seen on the house today was not added until 1903, when the entire exterior was refinished with brick. An elaborate copper gutter system carried rain and snow meltage from this roof to vertical downspouts, which in turn, tied into a main drain.

Off the northern end of the Westerly Extension, a circular, conical-roofed porch was built, its design similar to the one that still graced the house's southern end. Both porches had meticulously-joined exposed rafters, reminiscent of railroad depot work, and roofs laid with narrow white pine, planed face down so that those staring up could appreciate them.

Inside the house, plastering thousands of square feet of walls and ceilings required

*The front of the house from the carriage turnaround, ca. 1905*

weeks of work time. The crews trowelled on the traditional three coats — scratch coat, browning and hard white finish — over lath. The plaster consisted of "clean coarse sand, best quality lump lime, and long cattle hair mixed in their proper proportions."

Once the ceilings dried, specially skilled craftsmen executed the ornamental-plaster relief work in the Marble Room. Finish carpenters laid spruce floors, except in the Marble Room, and built two staircases with elegant balustrades and oak paneling. Installation of a variety of windows — casement, double-hung, fixed — followed thorough coats of lead paint on the sash and surrounds, which protected the wood from the weather. To ease the maids' job of opening the double-hung windows, they were equipped with lifting sash fit with "best quality Russia hempen, six strand sash cord, large size, noiseless pulleys, cast iron weights, etc., complete." Glass panes were specified double thick because of the weather. Finish casings for these windows stayed plain.

Interior doors were one and three-quarters inches thick, while more substantial doors to the outside were two and one-half inches of clear pine, paneled and moulded.

The exterior clapboards and trim were painted different tints of oil and lead paint. The second story shingles were stained. Robertson wisely ordered that samples of all

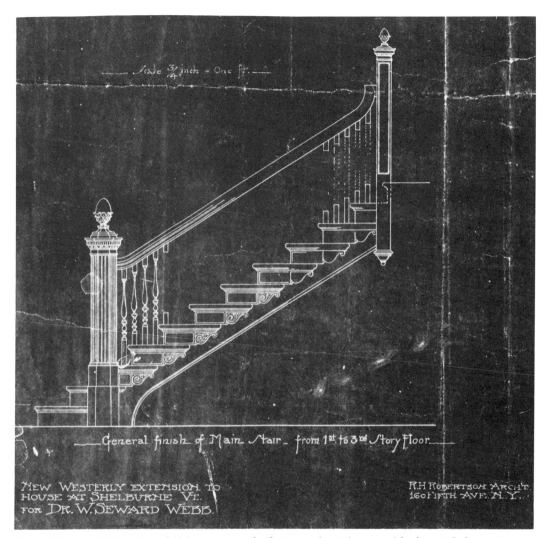

*From Robertson's blueprints, finish carpenters built two main staircases with elegant balustrades and oak paneling.*

the paint be shown to the Webbs before the application began.

The building of two new wings and the remodeling of the cottage into a harmonious whole required the labor of a lot of men. Crews of masons, carpenters, roofers, plasterers, along with their helpers and apprentices, came and went. Wagons hauled large loads of lumber, paint, fasteners, brick and numerous other materials to Saxton's Point. Being on the scene must have been exciting.

Slowly, the largest house in Vermont swallowed the former cottage and declared its dominance. It rivaled the residences of Newport and Bar Harbor, and signaled that the Webb family headquarters had caught up in size and grandeur with the estate over which it presided.

## Architectural Details

The main residence was completed in 1899. Architectural details, such as the conical-roofed porches, the tall, clustered chimneys, the octagonal tower juxtaposed to the earlier circular one, the variably-pitched roofs with their dormers and eyebrow windows, added to the impression of a solid complexity. There was, in the Queen Anne manner, a distinct absence of flat wall surfaces. Contrasting materials, projecting bays and towers, differently shaped windows — all helped to break up the flatness of thousands of square feet of wall.

As in the cottage, decorative details added to enhance visual appeal were relatively few. The gables remained half-timbered. The eaves and rakes were boxed in. Porch columns were solid looking, possibly because more delicately-turned supports and spindlework might have been overpowered by the house's size. There were dentils and brackets, particularly brackets. Ornate and plain, they knuckled around second story projections, gave massive support to cornice work, jutted out from beside dormer windows as embellishment, and lent strength to the superb rafter networks of both semi-circular porches. One interesting visual break between first and second stories, the cornice band separating the original lower clapboards from the upper shingles, was retained even when the facade was bricked in 1903.

Exactly why the Webbs had these clapboards and shingles removed and a brick facade laid up is a good question. Architectural historians would probably say this brick was a late Victorian look popular in the conservative Northeast. Just as likely, "They were getting zapped by the wind; the place was drafty and cold," Martin Tierney, project architect for the transformation of the house into an inn, speculates. Whatever the reason, there was some disgruntlement with the dramatically altered appearance of the house.

In a letter to Lila written in July, 1904, the masonry contractor tried politely to explain why the windows were now flush, or just about, with the brick exterior. Basically, he said, his crew had built out all window jambs and sills, replacing the latter with stone. The work was complicated, and, although he does not state it clearly, a certain visual proportion as seen from inside each room limited how wide jambs and sills could be. Evidently, his explanation sufficed. Nothing was done to alter this rather flush appearance that ran counter to the Queen Anne look of juxtaposed surfaces.

One subtle variation that did help delineate the brick surfaces of the first and second stories was new, however; first-story mortar was tinted, and second-story mortar was left natural.

The result of all this was a house that rambled both visually and physically. The unity of line and scale of the Shingle Style cottage, which had broken with more formal residences to the south, was foregone for eclectic grandeur. At the same time, the sense of potential for significant happenings, of scale commensurate with the estate as a whole, was greatly increased.

The layout of the interior reflected this

*The long western facade photographed on a moody autumn afternoon*

change in scale and potential even more significantly than did the exterior.

## Interiors

Gilded Age Victorians saw themselves as the embodiment of a Renaissance, an American Renaissance which combined and blended various historic styles into an exemplary new one. In architecture their models were medieval, in gardening Italian Renaissance, and for interiors, a mix of precedents representing wealth and power: Imperial Rome, Renaissance Florence, Bourbon Paris and Georgian England.

The resultant interiors made individual statements about house owners and their tastes. Rooms in a house differed dramatically. Often, a veritable chaos of styles and colors seemed to be in combat for the eye. Overstuffed sofas, fainting couches, chairs and side tables, rugs, photographs, art, palms and flowers filled every niche and wall and section of the floor.

Yet what designers today call clutter, Victorians of a hundred years ago saw as organized display rich with meaning, both personal and symbolic. A glance at photographs arranged in all styles of frame on a side table might identify family friends. Recent travels might be subtly suggested by memorabilia on a mantel. Things were

*Busts of philosophers and writers peered down from above some of the Library's six thousand volumes*

arranged to suggest the complexity and texture in the owners' lives.

To describe this complexity of style and display, the society novelist, Edith Wharton, and her co-author, architect and decorator, Ogdon Codman, Jr., in their book, *The Decoration of Houses*, coined a phrase from Victorian buzzwords: scientific eclecticism. The elements of this eclecticism were again historic, but emphasized a relaxed formality, a mix both natural and romantic. Proportion

and quality ranked foremost in importance. Original pieces of furniture were placed beside reproductions. Louis XVI and English Georgian styles gained favor. Color schemes for this scientific eclectic style brightened and simplified interiors which for decades had been dark and gloomy. Single colors and their shades unified a room, made it more pleasing, Wharton and Codman said.

The interior of the Webbs' house demon-

*The Conservatory*

Arriving by carriage at the completed house in 1901, a visitor still unloaded beneath the porte-cochère with its engraved capitals and timberwork ceiling. But the Main Hall, now much larger than before, paneled in oak and warmed in cool weather by a Tudor Style fireplace, suggested the overall change in the interior.

The Library off the hall had tripled in size. It now shelved six thousand volumes. Lila wrote her letters here and would later research her gardens from a collection of gardening reference books. On the parqueted floor sat sofas and comfortable chairs. Busts of philosophers and writers peered down at occupants from above the rows of book spines.

The cottage breakfast room and kitchen were now the Tea Room and part of a long, angular corridor leading to the Marble Room, the showcase of the Westerly Extension. Glassed on its lakeview side, and echoing the sound of a fountain in the adjacent Conservatory, this was the most formal room in the house. Family portraits hung on the walls. Plaster relief work ornamented ceiling beams. Marble serving tables complimented the marble floor. A large fireplace centered the northern wall and a carved bust of Medusa, the mythical female whose hair was snakes and whose stare turned those unlucky enough to

strated that this evolving aesthetic affected them, and that they did with it what they had done to the architecture and the landscape: they changed it to suit their tastes. This meant opulence giving way to comfort. Gilded Age socialites might see art treasures, priceless tapestries, and Chinese ceramics while visiting Lila's brother's Biltmore estate. But not here. The main house of the Webbs' working farm needed to be elegant, but relatively informal, and it was.

The Industrial Age that provided the Webbs with their money also ushered in an array of machine goods on which to spend it. A selection of furnishings, china, utensils and bric-a-brac hardly imagined before became suddenly and abundantly available. Machine-made meant high quality; it was prized. These new material things collected and displayed by the Webbs were another element identifying who they were and what they liked.

*An ornate, plaster-cast ceiling, damask wall covering, marble serving tables, and the adjacent Conservatory filled with orchids and palms made the Marble Room the most formal in the house.*

*The Tea Room, used for breakfast and informal dinners, connected the Main Hall with the Marble Room*

look at it into stone, crowned the mantel. The dining room table seated twelve, although the room could easily handle three times that number.

Dr. Webb's Game Room completed the first floor of the Westerly Extension. Here, an imposing blend of Elizabethan, Renaissance and Rococo design elements all added up to an aura of weighty authority. Amidst cigar smoke and clicking billiard balls, it must have provided the right ambience for making business deals and planning hunting trips. Trophies from the doctor's game trips stared at each other with glassy eyes, making an interesting counterpoint to the busts in Lila's Library at the opposite end of the house.

One small but unique space on the first floor was the Golf Room. Lined with lockers filled with clubs, it opened out toward the Shelburne Farms Golf Links, the third such course in the country. James Fox of Pennsylvania had introduced the game to the United States in 1885, following a visit to Scotland. Now the Webbs and their guests, as well as certain upper-rank servants like Woodgate the steward, challenged their skills on the nine hole course of three thousand and ten total yards with a par of thirty-six strokes.

Throughout the house the feel was affluent, but informal by Victorian stan-

*The Rose Room. The Webb's eldest child, and only daughter, Frederica, decorated her room with photographs of family and friends.*

dards. Furniture ranged from institutional to reproductions to Baroque to Chippendale. Art decorated the walls, but not priceless art. Photographs and travel memorabilia and purchased goods were arranged and displayed. Portraits of the families, on both Vanderbilt and Webb sides, lined walls. Butlers and maids moved over rugs and down corridors. The air smelled of fresh flowers from the greenhouses.

The upper floors were reached by the oak staircase off the Main Hall and by a second staircase located between the Game Room and the Marble Room. Bedrooms, closets, a large nursery space, a playroom for the children, and long, wide corridors occupied these two floors. The decor of the bedrooms varied tremendously, from the girlish Rose Room, where Frederica arranged her favorite photographs on flowery wallpaper, to the Dutch Room, which had a fireplace surround of tiles depicting scenes in Holland, ancestral home of Jan van der Bilt. The Brown Room, the Lilac, Cherry and Grey

*After dinner Dr. Webb and his male friends retired to the Game Room for cigars, port and billiards. Ornate, eclectic and masculine, the room provided the right atmosphere for discussing business deals and planning sporting trips.*

*Overlook, Lila's room, gave her a fine view of her gardens bordering the lake. The elaborate window coverings — hooded lambrequins, drapes and curtains — were typical of the era.*

*Baths were tiled, fixtures massive, and lavatory handles sculptural*

her dressing table and writing desk.

The third story contained more bedrooms similarly furnished and decorated, as well as the Play Room for the children. Large, airy and well lit, the Play Room housed the children's toys and several large dollhouses, which looked quite similar to the original Shingle Style cottage, with miniature shingles on the roofs and second stories, and with clapboards below. Small bedrooms off to either side of the Play Room provided sleeping quarters for the younger children, both the Webbs' and their guests, and for the nurses who watched the youngsters.

No description of the interior does the house justice without mention of the baths. Unique, although similar in appointments — massive tubs, stainless fixtures, porcelain handles, white tile floors, shoulder height tiles on the walls — the baths radiated a sense of luxury. Solid, sensuous lavatories balanced on thick pedestals. Water was let in by an array of almost sculptural faucet handles. Some tubs rested on claw feet, others on ceramic squares, some sat on the tiles. Casement windows with diamond motifs cast elongated patterns of shadow across the white porcelain surfaces. Toilets were a mix of elevated tank types and standards. These bathrooms promised deep, luxurious baths, bubbles swelling up out of the thick steam.

Rooms all featured monochromatic color schemes. Tints of the dominant color could be seen in the rugs, drapes, bedspreads and, in some of the rooms with fireplaces, in the tiles of the surround.

The second floor hallway was done in a popular late Victorian look: light colored woodwork and red flock wallpaper. On tables and in corners stood palms and vases filled with freshly cut flowers.

At the southern end of this hallway, fanning off from the top of the main stairway, were Dr. Webb's Room and Lila's Overlook. Both bedrooms displayed a mix of furniture styles. A massive rosewood bed dominated the doctor's quarters. He wrote at a desk made of fiddleback maple, and country Currier and Ives prints decorated his walls. In Overlook, Lila slept beneath an elaborately hooded drapery. On her walls hung personal photographs. Flowers in vases added color and a touch of the gardens to

*A synopsis of accounts, 1906. Note that carriage expenses exceeded automobile ones three times over. And taxes cost roughly the same amount as the Golf Links maintenance.*

# Making the House Function: The Servant System

It is the organization of the Victorian country house plan which remains their most fascinating aspect. They were enormous, complicated and highly articulated machines for a way of life that seems as remote as the stone age...
— Mark Girouard,
*The Victorian Country House*

At its peak the house at Shelburne Farms was many things: family home, resort hotel, business headquarters for railroad interests, figurative hub of a model farm, and dormitory for a staff of thirty and more, depending on how many guests were present. A bizarre combination of responsibilities, the house required expensive support and maintenance, and a lot of it. This servant system was to the house what a horse was to a carriage: it made it go. And in this house, as in most others where American wealth could afford a servant hierarchy, the system was based on English models.

An almost military rank existed. Duties were rigorously defined. Servants were dressed, fed and boarded, and often spent their whole lives working for the family. A number of them would retire on the estate and live out their lives here.

Overseeing this operational staff was not the butler, a figure who has come down to modern times as the functional household head, honest to his employers, feared by his inferiors, privy to goings on great and small, and exemplar of correct conduct at all times, but the steward—in this case, Walter Woodgate. A tall, stately Englishman, Woodgate had received his early training at Blenheim, home of the Dukes of Marlborough and the estate where Winston Churchill was born. Woodgate ran the "Big House," as the staff called it. He managed the servants, appraised their performances, and made sure that transfers from one house to another went smoothly and effortlessly for the family. He also hired new people, fired those remiss in their duties, and managed the household accounts.

*Victorian valets dressed very much like their employers. Here, Tom Macintee, Dr. Webb's valet, gives the man a hand. The unidentified fellow on the right was probably the chauffeur.*

Among Woodgate's subordinates were the butler and the footmen, the housemaids, the kitchen staff — including the cook, although this position was almost unto itself — and later, when autos replaced carriages, the chauffeurs. These subordinates lived their own scheme of protocol, which was status conscious, mannered and based on the lives of their employers, and often worked for decades, traveling frequently with the Webbs to New York City, to Nehasane lodge and game park in the Adirondacks, or abroad.

While at Shelburne Farms these servants lived in a large wing attached to the main house. This warren of rooms stood two stories and was built in a modest Queen Anne Style, with cross gables and tall Tudor chimneys jutting above the roof of the kitchen area. It was shielded from the view of arriving guests by a grove of cedar trees planted tight to the eastern facade.

The functional core of the wing took up considerable space where the structure abutted the main house and the Westerly Extension. Here were the kitchen, pantries, storage, larder and refrigeration rooms. An important technological feature of the times was mounted in this area, a buzzer system for calling servants to any room. Fitted in a well-trimmed wooden cabinet, this system included revolving arrows that pointed up at the name of the room in which the butler's presence was required, the arrow being activated by a button in the wall of the respective room.

As Victorian morality dictated, male and female accomodations in the wing were separated. The men lived on the first floor. The women occupied the second. Their bedrooms were each ten feet by twelve feet, and flanked a long hallway. For these parlormaids and housemaids, access to the second story of the Big House was through a corridor past shared baths and a room with a fireplace — possibly that of the head housekeeper, always a formidable figure. They entered the Big House near the Yellow Room.

The wing was kept up-to-date, and catered to the family and their guests' every need. To facilitate service, there was an elevator from the cellar to the second story. Refrigerator rooms kept meat and game frozen. The two-storied Ice House, some thirty foot square and equipped with its own elevator, was packed each February with huge blocks cut from Lake Champlain. Blanketed in sawdust insulation, these blocks of ice awaited their tour of duty.

Of all the rooms in the wing, the kitchen was the largest and most impressive. About twenty feet wide and forty feet long, it had a tile floor, wooden storage cabinets, marble wainscotting and a big stove. A bay window provided good lighting. The servants' dining room was down several marble steps on one side of the room. On the other side, up marble steps and through double swinging doors, was the Butler's Pantry.

By 1899, when the Big House was finished and fully functioning, the servant system worked smoothly, like a well lubricated machine. A big machine. These servants had their own quarters, ate well, and, although they worked six and a half days a week, had come a long way from the popular mid-century image of overworked drudges sleeping beside the stove in the kitchen. Some estates became so big and complex though, so intent on a kind of complicated perfection, that fortunes went into supporting the requisite staff. These unwieldy Victorian relics succumbed to their own weight.

In the house at Shelburne Farms this was never the case. For a residence of this size, with its interlocking demands — heat, food, service, transportation, business, pleasure — thirty servants was not an unwieldy number. It can safely be said also that none of them were forced to crouch in small anterooms and come running at the beck and call of the master, as had some of their predecessors in England. Nor did the liveried footmen have to lug preferred family beds wherever the Webbs traveled.

Eccentric behavior in the upper classes, standard and oddly charming with English Victorians, wasn't the custom in rural Vermont. Duties here were a bit more practical.

These duties began early in the morning for the parlormaids, who wore floor length dresses, starched aprons and small white caps. Depending on the weather, there were fires to set, or shutters to be opened, or drapes to be arranged, or, if the weather was mild, screens to be placed in dozens of windows. The gardeners brought in fresh flowers. In a room off the kitchen wilted blossoms were removed from the collected vases, and then the refreshed arrangements were carried back to all the rooms and hallways throughout the house.

Breakfast was taken with the other servants before the family was fed. Then, while the Webbs and any guests dined, the maids stripped and made the beds, brought towels, cleaned sinks and tubs. Later there were carpets to beat, furniture to polish, windows and mirrors to make gleam, hallways to sweep. Brass fire implements required shining. Floors frequently needed polishing on hands and knees. Hearths required cleaning after each use, and hearthstones needed to look as though they were whitewashed before new fires were set.

Luckily for these maids, the house was equipped with a mammoth coal furnace in the cellar, so fireplace heat was really supplementary. A network of pipes and ducts and airflow control boxes, which were labeled with the names of the rooms they supplied with hot air, crammed the ceiling and walls in the cellar. An ingenious combination of steam and hot air kept the one hundred rooms warm. Several men worked down there in the bowels of the house, making sure the heating, plumbing and electrical systems, all innovative for the age and controlled by motley valves, hand-operated levers and switches, worked like they were supposed to. When the temperature dropped, these men needed help keeping the furnace stoked; it consumed a coal car of fuel every few days in frigid weather.

Upstairs, bells were rung for the family's meals. The butler and footmen served the food after it was brought from the kitchen to their serving pantry.

Scrubbing was an unending routine. Kitchen help did the dishes and pots and pans. Footmen washed glassware. Silver was carried down a winding stairway to the Silver Cleaning Room, and when dried and not in use, put in the specially designed Mosler safe, inside of which there was a second and smaller safe, the function of which is not known. Between meals, everything in the kitchen and ancillary rooms gleamed.

Answering the door for guests, and directing the daily flow of meals and sport and pleasure possibilities, was the steward, Mr. Woodgate. Whenever he was otherwise detained, this job fell to the butler. Both men typically dressed in white shirts, waistcoats and jackets, pin-striped trousers and black shoes and socks.

The footmen assisted the butler in his serving duties, and also handled the considerable logistics of shuttling horses and carriages between the house and the Coach Barn over a quarter of a mile away. They saw to the travels of the family and others around the four thousand acres as well. Dressed in livery, the footmen tended to be young and strong and good with horses.

Closest to the master and madam of the house were her personal maid and his valet. The personal maid cared for her madam's toilet articles, laid out her clothes, woke her in the morning, took care of her bedroom and bath. Dr. Webb's valet lived up a narrow staircase directly above his master's bedroom. His responsibility was to see that the gentleman always appeared immaculate. Up before Dr. Webb, he laid out his clothes, brought his newspaper and coffee, and, when the doctor was in his prime, must have been an eager traveler who was adept at loading guns. Later in life, when his master was elderly and confined to a wheelchair,

the valet helped him with his meals, which he took in his quarters, and got him dressed.

## The Cook and Her Kitchen

Everything in the Big House was made from scratch: meat glazes, fish sauces, garnishes, desserts. The cook conferred with Lila on menus, but the outcome was her responsibility. And the numbers varied tremendously, from several members of the family to several dozen guests with their entourage of servants.

Being the cook was one of the most demanding jobs on the whole estate. A good cook was respected both by the family and by the other servants. She must have been an imposing sight in her white dress and apron, commanding a stove the size of a small battleship, footmen and kitchen maids awhirl about the tile floor, steaming dishes rushing up and out the swinging doors.

All her raw foodstuffs came in bulk from Burlington, or were grown on the farms. Vegetables, in season, were carted up daily from the gardens (some, out of season, were grown in the greenhouses). Milk, cream, eggs, butter came from the Farms. Animals were raised and slaughtered for beef, lamb, pork and poultry. Game was plentiful. Meals were a smorgasbord of offerings, all in large quanities.

*The Coach Barn Tack Room*

Which leads to an interesting observation. The Webbs, in their many existing photographs, are trim. It seems unlikely they overindulged their appetites. Corpulent men and women cinched tightly in bodices might have been the norm in the cities, but not here in the country.

Nevertheless, to tempt themselves, for breakfast there were two or three hot dishes as well as cold ham and game. Lunch consisted of four or five courses, and dinner increased that number to seven or eight, and sometimes for special occasions, to nine. Lunch and dinner always included soup, fish and meat dishes, a sweet and a savory. When entertaining, the Webbs, as was customary, served wines and champagnes with the various courses.

## The Coach Barn and Carriages

A coach barn filled with carriages, horses, harnesses and support staff was an integral part of a country estate. The original such barn at Shelburne Farms was built not far from the Shingle Style cottage, but it was later dismantled and a second, more elaborate one followed in 1901.

Designed by architect Robert H. Robertson around an interior courtyard, this complex was south of the house about a quarter of a mile, and close to the lake. Measuring

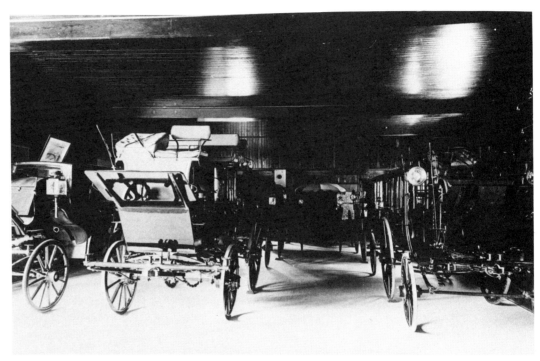

*Some of the eighty-odd carriages stored in the Coach Barn*

a hundred and sixty feet by a hundred and ninety feet, it was entered through an arched gateway. The courtyard was seventy-five feet by a hundred feet, and decorated with a clocktower. From its cobblestones, muddy carriages could be rolled into the wash room straight ahead. Harnesses could be taken to the harness-cleaning room, and horses led to their stalls which were brick walled and trimmed with wrought iron. The interior of the large room containing the thirty-two closed stalls (there were also sixteen roomier, open ones) was finely trimmed in wood, as were the harness and carriage rooms.

Carriages were stored in the wings on each side of the courtyard or, if less in demand, were wheeled to the elevator for storage upstairs. Grooms, the Coach Barn supervisor, and other help lived up there in thirteen sleeping rooms. In addition, there

*The Coach Barn in 1901, as it neared completion. Originally closer to the house, it was moved farther away and enlarged after work ceased on the main residence.*

and off they trotted, pulling a pony cart.

The numbers of carriages and sleighs Dr. Webb collected and used were indicative of his passion for horses. He owned sporting village carts in which passengers rode side-by-side, their positions over the axle adjustable for weight and forward body lean. There were stylish gigs, perfect for hackneys to carry one quickly to town or to the station. There were four-wheeled carriages, like the enclosed park drag, and runabouts and phaetons and miniature carts for the children, as well as all kinds of work and service and specialty wagons.

An entire world of saddlery, of blinders, brass rings and studs, of backpads and exotic bits and traces, of little men called "tigers," who perched high on the rears of racing rigs while adding very little weight, existed to move the wealthy about, most of it stranger to us today than the far side of the moon. When two horses pulled a roadster, the first was the lead, the second the wheeler. Driving a four-in-hand, something Dr. Webb savored, one held the reins to all four animals in the left hand, a whip in the right; it was not a maneuver for those lacking confidence in their commands. In wintertime, drivers climbed down from their sleighs, snowball hammers in hand, and unclogged horseshoes for a better grip on ice and rolled snow.

was a large, comfortable sitting room for the help on duty awaiting a call from the house. A hay loft and grain bins with chutes to facilitate feeding were also on the second story. The network was heated by steam from large boilers in the cellar.

Outside the four wings and their enclosed courtyard was an open shed for storing the baggage wagons.

It was no simple matter getting a horse or carriage ready for someone wanting to leave the house. When a phone call was made to the Coach Barn, horses were either saddled for riding or harnessed for a carriage. The vehicle was wheeled out and the traces hooked up. Driven beneath the broad arch, it had to travel another few minutes before arriving beneath the porte-cochère. If the request was for a less frequently driven vehicle, such as a brougham or the special picnic carriage kept upstairs, the elevator had to lower it. In winter, furs had to be arranged on the seats of sleighs, and if the outing was for pleasure, bells attached to harnesses. If the children were going for a ride, ponies were brought from their stalls

*Driving four-in-hand, one held the reins in the left hand and the whip in the right. Here, while four footmen calm the teams, Dr. Webb and James Watson prepare to leave the house driving in this challenging style.*

Carriage builders were numerous, and quality varied. For instance, Dr. Webb owned a Brewster Company four-wheeled runabout which cost $425, while a similar version from the more plebian Sears, Roebuck & Company went for $24.95.

For the wealthy, taking timed journeys over established routes was a sport they called Coaching. It was a way they added some stimulation to their often stilted lives. Handling spirited horses was exciting. Strict rules prevailed, and private clubs, to which one had to be elected, catered to gentlemen.

One of these, The Coaching Club, of which Dr. Webb was a founding member, twice journeyed from New York City to Shelburne Farms. The trip was a challenge for the horses, the equipment and the drivers as they traveled the timed course. It was also an abrupt change from offices and sumptuous dining rooms.

A photograph from the start of the 1894 trip shows Dr. Webb with seven friends on the top of his park drag, which was a fancy enclosed coach. The doctor sports a top hat, his friends wear bowlers. It is 8:30 a.m. and they are in front of the Hotel Brunswick in New York. The men seem animated, the horses calm. One of the men intends to play a little golf up north; his clubs dangle from a side of the carriage.

The trip was exceptionally long for The

## COACHING CLUB, NEW YORK TO SHELBURNE, VERMONT.
### June 6th to June 9th, 1894.

| Distance (Miles) | Time (A.M.) | RUTLAND, JUNE 9TH. | Team No. | Coachman. |
|---|---|---|---|---|
| | 9.00 | Bates House. | 14 | W. K. Vanderbilt. |
| 8 | 10.00 | *Pittsford. (Otter Creek House.) | 15 | W. K. Vanderbilt. |
| 8 | 11.00 | *Brandon. (Brandon House.) | 16 | O. H. P. Belmont. |
| 5 | 11.40 | *Leicester. | 17 | O. H. P. Belmont. |
| 5 | P. M. 12.20 | *The Thomas Farm. | 18 | E. V. R. Thayer. |
| 6 | 1.10 Arr. | *†Middlebury. (Addison House.) | 19 | W. C. Whitney. |
| | 2.10 Dep. | | | |
| 7 | 3.05 | *New Haven Depot. | 20 | W. S. Webb. |
| 5 | 3.50 | *Verjeunes. (Stevens House.) | 1 | W. S. Webb. |
| 6 | 4.40 | *North Ferrisburg. | 2 | W. S. Webb. |
| 6 | 5.20 | *Charlotte. (Old Road House.) | 3 | W. S. Webb. |
| 4 | 5.45 | Shelburne. | | |
| 3 | 6.00 | Shelburne Farms. | | |
| 63 | | | | |

\* Changes.  † Luncheon on Car " Ellesmere."

## COACHING CLUB. NEW YORK TO SHELBURNE, VERMONT.
### June 6th to June 9th, 1894.

| Distance (Miles) | Time (A.M.) | NEW YORK, JUNE 6TH. | Team No. | Coachman. |
|---|---|---|---|---|
| | 8.30 | Hotel Brunswick. | 1 | W. S. Webb. |
| 10½ | 9.45 | * Kingsbridge. | 2 | W. S. Webb. |
| 6½ | 10.35 | *2 m. N. of Yonkers. (Saw Mill Valley Road.) | 3 | W. S. Webb. |
| 9 | 11.25 | *Tarrytown. (Franklin House.) | 4 | A. J. Cassatt. |
| 6½ | P. M. 12.10 Arr. | *†Sing Sing. (American House.) | 5 | A. J. Cassatt. |
| | 1.10 Dep. | | | |
| 5½ | 1.50 | *North Croton. Cyrus Frost's Farm, (2 m. N. of Croton Station.) | 6 | F. K. Sturgis. |
| 5½ | 2.30 | *Peekskill. (Eagle House.) | 7 | F. Bronson. |
| 8 | 3.40 | *Garrisons. (Highland House.) | 8 | T. A. Havemeyer. |
| 7 | 4.25 | *Davenports Corners. | 9 | T. A. Havemeyer. |
| 6½ | 5.10 | *Fishkill. | 10 | P. Lawrence. |
| 5 | 5.40 Arr. | Carnwath. | | |
| | 5.50 Dep. | | | |
| 3 | 6.10 | *Wappingers Falls. | 11 | R. W. Rives. |
| 8 | 7.00 | Poughkeepsie. (Nelson House.) | | |
| 82½ | | | | |

\* Changes.  † Luncheon on Car " Ellesmere."

BLACK, STARR & FROST, PRINT.

*Coaching in Victorian times captivated the attention of wealthy gentlemen. Over timed courses, carriages and teams competed under strict rules. Here, the card (showing only the start and end of the course) from a four-day trip taken in 1894 by The Coaching Club of New York, lists the drivers, stops and intended elapsed times between New York City and Shelburne Farms.*

Coaching Club, their jaunts more often restricted to Central Park or courses nearer the city. The horses needed to be well matched in temperament, strength and nerves. This was a test as much for the skill of Dr. Webb's coachman, Charles Welch, who bought and paired the teams, as for the drivers. They traveled up through Yonkers and Tarrytown, then to Peekskill and Wappingers Falls, taking turns driving, changing teams, dining in Dr. Webb's private rail car, the *Ellesmere*, which kept pace along nearby tracks. After Albany and Troy, on the morning of the third day, they entered Vermont near Bennington, and then came up a route that was the predecessor of today's U.S. Route 7, arriving at Shelburne Farms at 6:00 p.m. on the fourth day. The total distance through towns, over rivers and hills, through rain and sunshine, was three hundred and eighteen miles. It must have been fun.

*Lila and her two eldest children, Frederica and James Watson, pose informally by the porte-cochère.*

# A Country Estate Lifestyle

Life in the Big House was refreshingly informal for the time. The Webbs filled their rooms with furniture, plants, books and memorabilia, as was the fashion, yet the selections were neither for show nor boastful ornamentation. Decorative interiors were chosen from those readily available. The Webbs did not collect art.

This relaxed lifestyle was much different from the stiff one at Hyde Park, Frederick Vanderbilt's very formal French Empire Style estate, or the heavily cultural lifestyle at Biltmore in North Carolina, where brother George collected art, antiques and tapestries. It is doubtful that either of these brothers of Lila's, or other friends with country places, allowed sheep to graze the front lawn, or erected a toboggan run in front of the house during the winter. The Webbs certainly affected similar manners, dress and conduct, but the degree to which these societal mores were honored was much relaxed up north.

The turn-of-the-century America the Webbs inhabited was a place we would hardly recognize: no income taxes, no cars, no radio or television, no vote if you were female. A father's authority to determine his family's direction was unquestioned. A wife, on the other hand, lived a circumscribed existence. She needed to be hospitable, competent in managing a large house, and supportive of her husband. Graciousness was much praised. Bearing the children was of course her responsibility, but their rearing was left primarily to nurses.

Although few letters or journals survive to substantiate the doctor and Lila's feelings about this society and their roles in it, it seems they were not discontent. Far north of their relatives and wealthy peers, yet in constant contact through letters and via the railroad, they carried on a rural lifestyle familiar yet different, elegant but relatively informal, a long way away and yet easily accessible by rail. The way they lived must have both intrigued and perplexed their friends. Ultimately, their style seemed quite their own.

In dress, the doctor affected the popular

clean-cut look, hair short and brushed back, his moustache and goatee substantial but neat. He favored tweeds for daily informal wear, and jodhpurs, a waistcoat and boots while on horseback. Photographs suggest a military bearing in civilian attire: ramrod straight, attentive, he stares directly ahead. Lila wore dresses that reached to the ground, with long sleeves and high collars. A bonnet or hat was usually perched on her long hair. Such tresses were admired by most women of her class, their maids spending hours stroking them with a brush. But they were never left free in public. For colder weather Lila had a selection of capes, muffs and coats of sable, seal and velvet.

Conduct for the Webbs and most Victorians was determined by sex. Biology was fate. Women looked pretty, dressed well, visited and occasionally wrote of their frustrations as unsettling aberrations.

One youthful visitor who had trouble with this concept of a woman's role was Lila's niece, Adele Sloan. She wrote about it in letters and a diary.

A noted beauty listed in Mrs. William Astor's famous "Four Hundred," who were the elite members of New York's high society, Adele had cultivated the typical skills desired in a Gilded Age ingenue: foreign languages, piano playing, art appreciation, before falling in love with the forester Gifford

*Dr. Webb and a friend at Nehasane, the family game park in the Adirondacks*

Pinchot, then twenty-six, while visiting George Vanderbilt's Biltmore estate in 1892. The young woman was eighteen.

After that she struggled with feelings few of her friends seem to have shared. She grew weary of balls and travel and declarations of love from flatulent men.

Writing to Pinchot, who had finished his work for Dr. Webb and was undertaking an American first at Biltmore, a thorough forestry plan, Adele said she didn't believe there had been any woman geniuses yet and that her life seemed to be humdrum like most others she knew. Sneaking upstairs from a party, she wrote, "I am sitting at my desk and looking idly out on the ocean, and counting the stars and wasting my time wondering what I shall do." She tells him she hates the formality and the gossip. She desires experience and real things. She wants to travel, see poverty, sickness and sorrow to see what they are like. She writes:

> I have lived and seen only one side of life, and merely read and imagined the other. And it is difficult to understand and sympathize with what I know so little about... There is such selfishness connected with everything we do. Why is it that that feeling of self always seems to haunt one?

She concludes a little further on, "When one is only beginning to realize what it means to live, life seems very serious, and not to be laughed and jested away."

Adele's private writings reveal a woman trying to make sense of why she is unhappy when she has everything. One gets the feeling a pleasure dome is cracking about the edges. Her honesty is admirable, her continued frustration and inability to relieve it disconcerting.

Contemplating a trip north to Aunt Lila's in Vermont, Adele wonders if Pinchot might be at Shelburne Farms. She will go there for rounds of parties with nephews, nieces and friends. There will be winter diversions, such as fishing, tobogganing, riding. One wonders if she opened her heart to Lila, expressing her longing for the masculine, visionary forester who had worked for Dr. Webb, and if Lila, despite her traditionalism, was moved by the younger woman's loneliness and sense of constricted desperation. Pinchot, for his part, seems never to have been that serious about Adele; her expectations of seeing him at Shelburne Farms in 1893 were overly optimistic; he never came.

Most gentlemen of the times were not like the woodsman Pinchot. They had industries to run. They worked at business careers related to these industries, but seldom so zealously they could not hunt animals and travel to exotic places.

A personal code of honesty, conscientiousness, patriotism and family devotion was cultivated in men and women, as well as in their children. And despite the parties and travels and endless flirting, fidelity and faithfulness were cherished. Divorces and affairs were not unknown, however, and the press loved any hint of scandal amidst the ranks of the rich.

Manners were inbred. Charm, a facility with the social graces, affability and politeness were taught to children at an early age. Sullenness, being rude, and radical behavior were all discouraged, particularly in girls. Not that all the desired character traits showed up in succeeding generations of adults, rebellion against parental standards always having been a streak in the American temperament regardless of era. But genteel manners did reach an apogee in this country at the end of the 1800s.

The four Webb children, Frederica, James Watson, Seward, Jr., and Vanderbilt, who were eighteen, sixteen, thirteen, and eight respectively in 1900, spent the majority of their childhood years in the Shingle Style cottage and then in the Big House. Their lives were much different from the lives of most children, although the attitude towards their upbringing was conventional Victorian — they were seen as miniature adults, a concept that limited displays of affection

*Lila (with the feather in her hat), and the four children out riding on the estate*

between parents and children unless the latter were ill.

Children's lives tended to be over-dramatized as well, filled with elaborate replicas of adult playthings and events, but on a smaller scale, as though little people should enjoy what big people enjoyed, but orchestrated or built to fit their size.

For instance, a dollhouse, complete with miniature furniture, a stove and a sink, as well as a more adult-sized fireplace so the nurses could keep the children warm, was erected adjacent to the house. Once they

reached adolescence, the boys had carts and gentle teams of ponies so they could travel about the estate. Before the age of thirteen, James Watson, Seward and Van each learned to hunt, trap, ride and play polo. Their instructors were men on the Webb staff and seldom their father. Frederica rode well herself, but while her brothers checked their traps for muskrat, she was expected to be reading, practicing the piano, or studying her lessons.

Frederica wore ruffles and bonnets as a little girl, her hair bunched and ribboned.

The boys frequently wore the sailor suits that Victorian parents found so adorable on their children. Knickers, knee socks, bloused shirts and caps were also popular. As teen-agers the boys dressed much like their father — that is, informally, preferring loose trousers and tweed sport coats. When Frederica became a young woman, she wore the trim, attractive gowns of the era, gowns with long sleeves and with hems that brushed the ground. And she owned an array of stylish hats, of course.

Constant travel must have seemed as natural to these children as having servants. And must have occurred so smoothly as to have bordered on magic. Out-of-sight adults arranged the logistics. Rendezvous occurred punctually. One got whisked from school, or away from home, almost effortlessly. For the children of a railroad baron, possibly it seemed quite ordinary to spend so much time in luxurious quarters on rails.

All four of them went away to private schools before the age of ten. When away from school during the academic year, each was tutored privately.

The acquiring of athletic skills was part of this tutoring. And good horsemanship and marksmanship were as important in the scheme of things as were the more tradi-tional disciplines like reading and writing.

## Vanderbilt Webb's Diary: The View at Twelve

The youngest son, Vanderbilt, who would go on to be an attorney in New York, and in 1936 inherit (with his three siblings) the Big House, kept a fascinating diary in 1903 and 1904 when he was approaching that breakwater of a boy's life: thirteen. The opening entry on January 1, 1903, begins, "I had seen old year out the night before so I slept till 12 then got up & had lunch at one."

Van, as he is called, goes on to give a few details of his day. The writing is large and florid, double-spaced. The eleven year old pencils in a few sentences every day. He has a routine that varies. His activities include hunting, checking his traps, driving his ponies, playing polo in the Breeding Barn with his brothers, and just fooling around, which he does often. He reads a lot, and writes. Just as the entries get a bit repetitious he packs up and travels off somewhere.

Van Webb travels more in six months than the average American of his era did in a lifetime. He is constantly taking trains to New York City and to Nehasane in the Adirondacks, and from New York east to Groton School in Massachusetts, and then from there (he never stayed very long at school) back to Shelburne again.

Over the winter and into the spring, the diary suggests that paternal relationships between the boy and several servants are developing. Mr. Woodgate, the steward, takes him for walks in Central Park, and plays golf with him often in Vermont. The steward seems throughout this record of their golf matches to have intimidated Van at his usually good game; he always plays poorly with the man, and frequently quits after the sixth hole to stalk home. One of the farm staff, a Mr. Stillwell, is kindly spoken of: Mr. Stillwell repeatedly takes Van for "bully" and "corking" good rides, he poles the boy up branches of rivers flowing into Lake Champlain so he can hunt birds.

Though Van studies a lot, he does not go to school very often. It is easy to see why. During 1903 he takes six round trips to Shelburne from various locations, goes to Nehasane three times, Groton School twice, travels west via New Orleans and San Antonio to California, where the family stays for a month, and then in June, steams to England on the S.S. Teutonic.

This three-month jaunt about the continent produces not only an expanding awareness and a sense of drama in the young man, but markedly improves his ability to communicate it on the written page. Entries now fill the pages in an easily decipherable handwriting that both understates and dramatizes. With his parents and Frederica, he checks into the Carlton in London, motors around France, and wanders the streets of Paris hunting for balloons. ("Sounds foolish, doesn't it?" he writes as an aside). In Switzerland, he gets wet to the skin in an open car, and writes of water in the petrol and of repeated punctures in the

*Lila and her youngest son, Vanderbilt*

tires. Throughout he gives delightfully detailed and innocent glimpses of his experiences as though they were the common lot of all twelve year olds.

By the time he returns to Shelburne, the diary has taken on new dimensions: it reveals rather than categorizes. Van now seems to be almost a young man, excited with his potential, taking in gulps of life's action. On September 7, 1903, he writes:

> Went over to the Breeding Barns in the four-in-hand with Watson, Sissy, Seward and Mr. Stillwell where we got on our horses and started out with the beigles [sic]. They struck the drag just behind the Breeding Barns and started out and gave us a bully gallop all through the paddocks back of the Breeding Barns and all around the Old South Drive over 15 fences and 2 water jumps [and] then [we] came back and had dinner.

He describes quiet rides as well, and rounds of golf with his Mamma, who beats him, two up. He again tries his luck on the links with Woodgate and plays "so rottenly that I was ashamed to keep score."

In October he loads shells for one of the six hunters gunning the Farms' pheasant out of the sky. Dr. Webb and Sissy join them in the afternoon. The daily total is "500 pheasants, a fox and a hawk, a record!"

He plays squash, brings his golf score below sixty-five, rides and jumps inside the Breeding Barns in November, then returns to Groton briefly where he attends a Yale-Harvard football game, which he says with the bands, the crowd, the singing and cheering, was "awfully exciting."

Back at the house in late October, he catches chicken pox and lies on his back in bed, doing nothing. Lila reads *The Last of the Mohicans* and *The Call of the Wild* to him. A doctor visits daily. He gets better and is quickly back skating, playing hockey, checking his traps with Mr. Stillwell and playing golf with Woodgate in a snowstorm that drives them off the greens. On Christmas Eve there is Japanese entertainment, which he thinks is great.

Interestingly enough, the young Van Webb doesn't tell what his Christmas gifts were. In fact, throughout the diary, in which he writes every day, he maintains a fine, understated style and never stoops to describe things he owns or has received. Two exclamation points can be found in three hundred and sixty-five days worth of entries; one when the record number of farm-raised pheasant were shot, and the second when a laborer backed his team of horses into the lake off the coal dock, drowning both the animals and himself.

That year the boy listed twenty-two titles under the heading, Books I Have Read, at the rear of the diary. These included Rudyard Kipling's *The Jungle Book* and Robert Lewis Stevenson's *Treasure Island*.

The diary loses his attention, unfortunately, once he is back at Groton School in the Fall of 1904. The entries dwindle to repetitive phrases: School. Football. Evening School. School. And cease completely on October 20. Van Webb, the only Webb to be both raised in the house and to live a good portion of his adult life in it, was thirteen.

During these early years of the 20th century, when the Farms promised agricultural breakthroughs and a hackney in every farmer's harness, times were lively and fast paced. Frederica lived at home, as did Seward, Jr. and Van when not at Groton School. James Watson was off at college. Dr. Webb was testing the political turf with thoughts of making a run for governor (he withdrew eventually, unwilling to campaign aggressively for the nomination). These were the years when vice-president Teddy Roosevelt visited, and Admiral Dewey, a Vermont native and the hero of Manila in the Spanish-American War, rode beneath the porte-cochère aboard a four-in-hand driven by Dr. Webb, an awaiting crowd cheering heartily.

A typical day started then with breakfast in the Tea Room. Afterwards, Lila saw to sport and pleasure offerings Shelburne Farms made available to family and guests.

If it was spring, these included hunting, horseback riding and golf. In the summer there was yachting, tennis, croquet, more golf and riding. In the fall polo and hunting broadened the already numerous options. With snow came ice boating, skating, tobogganing and coasting. Throughout the year one could fish or go for carriage rides. Later there would be the Shelburne Farms Hunts,

> Some of the ladies had side saddles. I remember them, watching them, their skirts on the outside, going by the door.
>
> — Armande Boisvert, resident of the Farms since age ten.

*In front of the Breeding Barn, three riders and a pack of hounds await the start of a fox hunt*

special house duties with Mr. Woodgate and went over the lunch and dinner menu with the cook. Dr. Webb took care of business from an office in the rear of the servants' wing, where he had a direct telegraph line to Wall Street. In mid-morning, he might ride over to the Farm Barn to check with the manager, or visit the Breeding Barn. The Pheasantry, Poultry Barn and Boat House routinely required the presence of the master of the estate as well.

Lunch was served in the Marble Room by the butler and liveried footmen.

Afternoons were for enjoying the many where men and women on horseback chased foxhounds who chased a fox all over the farm acreage and the acreage of adjoining farms. There was a squash court in the annex, and a billiard table in the Game Room. Games of chance and mental skill were also popular: dice, marbles, Parcheesi and the old mainstay, checkers.

Shelburne Farms Links, the estate's nine hole golf course and the third such construction in the country, meandered for three thousand and ten yards between the pleasure grounds of the house and the functional landscape of meadows and greenhouses. Par was thirty-six strokes. The locker room in the house led to the first tee. One drove past Edward Saxton's remaining apple trees and played the fairways east towards Lone Tree Hill. Lila was an avid golfer, and hired caddies from the village. She and her friends wore long dresses and hats on the links, parasols shading their faces when the summer days were bright and hot.

In the autumn, hunters came to the house with their entourages. They quickened life there, as their servants quickened life in the servants' wing. Beaters were retained, valets compared their skills at loading shotguns, the lakeside air rang with gunfire. When the hunters departed, the refrigeration rooms were stocked with birds.

Dr. Webb enjoyed hunting more than the other options. Lila preferred golf. All four children loved to ride horses. Skating and hockey and polo received their share of attention. During winter holidays, when as many as thirty guests occupied the bedrooms, the toboggan run built between the house and the lake attracted all ages in all manner of warm attire. The thrill of each ride down the ramp and then down the hill depended, as always, on the nature and accumulation of the snow.

*A bird hunter on the lakeshore near the house*

*Tobogganing anyone? Dr. Webb (front row), Lila (second row, third from right), their children and friends all participated in this popular winter sport. Appropriately enough, the wooden trestle suggests a railroad bridge.*

## The Steam Yacht Elfreida

Steam yachts were both sport and pleasure showpieces in the Gilded Era, and the Webbs could provide their guests an ideal location for taking full advantage of these sumptuous mechanical toys. The story of Dr. Webb's yachts also illuminates the man's competitiveness and need to have the best.

On moving to Vermont, he brought his hundred and four foot long *Sappho* from New York, a steam yacht capable of thirteen miles per hour. A boathouse for the craft and its crew of eight, and a dock, were built on Quaker Smith Point during the construction of the original Victorian cottage.

In 1888, a Major W.B. Wetmore challenged the doctor to a race on Lake Champlain, the course running from Schuyler reef buoy to a point inside the breakwater. Dr. Webb accepted and Wetmore proceeded to soundly trounce the newly arrived Vermonter's *Nymph*, a yacht that had replaced the *Sappho*. The doctor blamed his defeat on damp coal and the resultant poor head of steam and decided he needed a new yacht.

So in 1889 he had Harlan & Hollingsworth of Wilmington, Delaware, make him the *Elfreida*, an impressive craft for cruising inland waters. Manned by a captain and a crew of fifteen, this steam yacht was schooner rigged. She had a steel hull, an engine capable of fifteen miles per hour, and two breech-loading cannons for saluting fellow yachtsmen.

To deliver the craft to Lake Champlain, the crew sailed around the Maritime Provinces, down the St. Lawrence River, and then up the Richlieu River to the Chambly Canal, a distance of approximately two thousand miles. The longest boat ever brought through the canal, the *Elfreida* measured a hundred and seventeen feet from stem to stern, five feet more than any of the locks. Consequently, her bowsprit and aft rail had to be removed (they had been built accordingly), and her ballast lifted out. Then the Chambly Canal crew chief pumped extra water into the first lock, so the *Elfreida* just cleared the bottom, and twenty men and six teams of horses hauled the hundred and twenty-two tons of yacht into the next lock. Repeating this process through all the locks, they lifted the *Elfreida* seventy-four vertical feet, and Dr. Webb sailed her out onto the lake.

There, *Elfreida* not only carried an impressive load of sail on sixty-six and sixty-four foot masts, but protected the preferred Victorian pallor of fifteen guests beneath an awning running the entire length of the deck. For overnight cruises three staterooms, all done in mahogany, provided guests with accommodations. Each stateroom bath had a mosaic marble floor and walls of quartered cypress. Moved to take a moonlighted look at the lake and mountains, the men in their whites and ladies in their dresses could climb to a brass-railed roof deck above the captain's semi-circular chart house and enjoy the view.

At the outbreak of the Spanish-American War in 1898, Dr. Webb donated the *Elfreida* to the United States Navy, and ordered a duplicate built by Harlan & Hollingsworth. Subsequently, both the naval hero of that war, Admiral Dewey, and Teddy Roosevelt, who led his Rough Riders up San Juan Hill, visited and stayed at Shelburne Farms. Roosevelt, who came as vice-president in 1901, steamed from Burlington to Isle La Mott aboard the second *Elfreida* to address the Vermont Fish & Game League. Hardly had he left the rostrum when word arrived that President McKinley had been shot in Buffalo, New York.

On this dark occasion, E.F. Gebhardt, a man whose presence on the Webbs' staff resembled that of chief master sergeant in charge of just about everything, was on board the *Elfreida*. Taking charge, Gebhardt ordered Roosevelt steamed straight to Burlington, the president-to-be muttering this memorable sentence to an enquiring *Free Press* reporter on board: "I should admire this beautiful sunset...but I am in no condi-

*On the stern of the steam yacht* Elfreida, *some of the family enjoy an afternoon on Lake Champlain*

tion to enjoy it now."

This second version of the yacht served family and guests for years. Cruising out on the lake aboard such a craft had to be a memorable experience even for visitors jaded from prolonged exposure to Victorian excess. In 1905 the yacht functioned as a floating hotel for guests at the marriage of Frederica Webb and Ralph Pulitzer.

This marriage of the doctor's only daughter proved to be a glorified incident of wealth and power for New York society. Private Pullmans lined up at the station. Yachts anchored in Shelburne Bay. Eighteen carriages bedecked with footmen took guests from the house to Trinity Church in Shelburne. Frederica pledged her troth while kneeling on a pillow of diamonds that Lila had knelt on when marrying Dr. Webb. After the ceremony the bride and groom were driven to the house in a coach drawn

*Schooner rigged and with two cannons with which to salute fellow yachtsmen, the* Elfreida *measured a hundred and seventeen feet from stem to stern. Here, she docks off Saxton's Point, the house in the background.*

*Wearing her bride's dress of white satin cut en princesse, Frederica Webb poses with her wedding party by the porte-cochère on October 15, 1905. Her husband, Ralph Pulitzer, was the son of publishing baron, Joseph Pulitzer. Seward Webb Jr. sits on the rug. James Watson Webb is in second row, second from right.*

*Drawn by four white horses, the coach returning the newlyweds from the church enters the porte-cochère. James Watson and Seward, Jr., dressed in scarlet jackets trimmed with gold braid, white breeches, top boots and black skull caps, ride the near mounts.*

by four white horses, her gleeful younger brothers James Watson and Seward, Jr., riding the near mounts.

At the house a dining tent decorated the lawn. After the meal the newlyweds departed in a shower of rice aboard the coach, then transferred to the *Elfreida* which steamed to the yacht club in Burlington. The couple boarded a private car on a special train for Montreal. Several hundred guests, including Vanderbilts and Pulitzers and much of the upper crust of New York society, partied in the house and aboard both the *Elfreida* and the steamer *Vermonter*, which the Webbs had rented to expand their accommodations for the occasion.

# Lila's Love: The Gardens

*A gift from architect Stanford White, this piece of Italian statuary, a nymph straddling a fish out of whose open mouth a fountain spewed, centered a small pool in Lila's Wild Garden.*

The spirits of gardeners are full of optimism, goes an old adage. It seemed aptly expressed in the gardens of the Big House between the years 1912 and 1926, when Lila Webb designed, built and evolved the gardens from a rectangular parterre to a spontaneous, dramatic English cottage style where the personality of the gardener was expressed in her flowers.

Prior to 1912, beds of annuals, such as geraniums, salvia and alyssum planted in patterns formed the French parterre. This garden interrupted the dominant visual impression of a huge house floating on a carpet of green, an impression highly desirable at one time. Lila seems never to have approved of this rather stark look however, even broken up as it was with elm trees that softened the house's long horizontal facade. She refrained from altering the parterre for many years though, and satisfied her gardening desires with a Wild Garden cultivated just to the north of the lawn that sloped gradually toward the lake.

Her eventual decision to abandon the parterre for the Italian style came in 1911. A familiarity with the American Garden Revival Movement then in vogue, her travels in Italy that summer, from which she returned with statuary and tentative revision plans, and a long lingering desire to express herself horticulturally, seemed to have compelled the decision.

The following spring, Alec Graham, her head gardener, began work on Lila's version of what she had seen on Italian estates and in her large folio gardening books: period formal gardens, classical in their geometry yet informal in their varied plantings.

The new gardens greatly enlarged the parterre arrangement they replaced. Entered off the North Porch along a walkway, the gardens branched in different directions. Over two thousand feet of low brick wall separated flower beds, terraces and gardens of roses and violets. Statuary and benches graced the many paths. Close to the North Porch, a pergola draped in vines hugged an oval reflecting pool. A grand allée, which suggested an outdoor room

*Four views of the gardens. Clockwise, from top left: the lion head fountain and lily pond, the pergola, the terraces off the North Porch, and the balustraded overlook with its bay trees.*

defined by flowers, bordered the lawn in front of the terrace, and centered the design.

In 1914 two picturesque elements of the classic Italian-style garden completed Lila's plan: a fountain with a lily pond, and a balustraded overlook by the cliffs of the lake.

Water arched out of a lion's head and fell to the surface of the pond. There, beneath full-grown lilies, swam goldfish. Around the pond's perimeter were bearded iris, and off to either side young conifers. A little closer to the lake stood the balustrade, an elegant, curved, sensuous railing complimented along its length by bay trees in Italian pots.

One can imagine walking down through the terraces on a moonlit night. The rising scent of flowers and earth, the dew on the grass, the lake glimmering beyond the silhouetted balustrade and the lollipop-shaped bay trees. Gowns rustled. Hems lifted off the path. There may have been laughter, shoes taken in hand for a rush to the rail. Leaning there, the couples listened to the lake slapping stones below, then looked back over the lilies and the fountain towards the sprawling mass of the house, windows glowing, elms spreading their dark crowns above the roof.

A newly developed photo process recorded the gardens in color. These photos reveal the pergola as a focus of the arrangements. Open to lake breezes, sheltering

*Three acres of steam-heated greenhouses provided flowers, vegetables, fruits and palms year round*

palms, ferns and clematis vines that wove themselves around the columns, the pergola seemed to embrace the reflecting pool, in which younger members of the family liked to cool off. From the pergola one could see the upper gardens' blue salvia, tall phlox, campanulas and English boxwood pyramids, which were three and a half feet tall. To the west sprawled Lake Champlain, and possibly the steam yacht *Elfreida*, if family or guests were out for a day of it.

The gardening staff under Alec Graham lived in cottages near the greenhouses. In the fall before the first frost they moved the bay trees and English boxwood pyramids into special quarters there, and they shared the reasonably warm space with pots of azaleas. During the cold months new stock for spring plantings was cultivated in these greenhouses.

*A family portrait in the gardens, 1916. Front row, left to right: Lila O. Webb holding Barbara Webb; Samuel Webb, Electra Webb, Lila Webb, Frederica Webb, Derick Webb, W. Seward Webb III, Seward Pulitzer, Dr. W. Seward Webb. Back row, left to right: Electra Havemeyer Webb, Frederica Webb Pulitzer, Ralph Pulitzer, Gertrude Gaynor Webb, James Watson Webb, Aileen Osborn Webb, Osborn Webb, Wm. Seward Webb, Jr., Vanderbilt Webb.*

## The English Cottage Style

A liberating presence in the gardens of this era was the philosophy of an English painter turned horticulturalist, Gertrude Jekyll. Her writings encouraged gardeners to put personality and freedom in their choices of flowers and plantings, rather than continuing with the patterns and formality favored by most Victorians. Jekyll claimed to have spent half her life figuring out what to do in her gardens, and most of the second half figuring out how to do it. She also refuted the notion that flower gardening was easy. It was not, she wrote emphatically.

Lila's experience with her gardens gradually came under Jekyll's sway. And in some ways ran a parallel course. Lila, like Jekyll, came to gardening later in life, and then required some time to decide just what she wanted to do.

The Shelburne Farms' greenhouses had grown flowers, vegetables, palms, ferns, grapes and huge strawberries for several decades. But Lila had not taken advantage of their potential. Steam-heated, manned by experts, the greenhouses were capable of growing just about anything.

By 1912 a relaxation of Victorian formality allowed Lila to begin expressing herself, and she turned to Alec Graham and the greenhouses for her stock. Then slowly, over the following decade, she evolved the still rather stiff Italian style into something beautiful and quite free when she finally embraced Gertrude Jekyll and the English cottage style for her inspiration.

This popular style she finally adopted had come a long way from the horizontal patterns of the parterre. The cottage style championed spontaneity, harmony and individuality. Less grandiose than its predecessors, it made up in exuberance and fun what it lacked in formality. Jekyll's theories, which were loosely impressionistic, had established the standards. In a phrase, she wanted gardeners to create paintings with flowers, to replace pigments with petals. Gardeners should enjoy themselves, she wrote. Vary plantings annually (seasonally, if they could afford it), and create something visually pleasing.

Pleasing herself, Lila mixed hollyhocks, phlox, foxglove, delphinium, lilies, peonies, campanula, coreopsis, roses, irises and others. Just to the north, and centered by an evocative piece of Italian statuary depicting a nymph straddling a fish (a gift of architect Stanford White), she continued to work her original experiment in this more personal style in the Wild Garden.

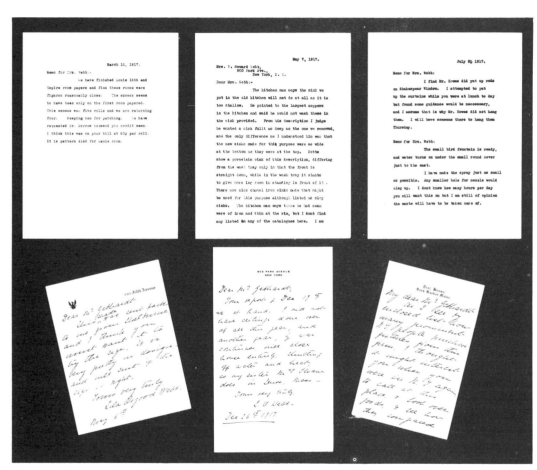

*Memorandums from E.F. Gebhardt to Lila Webb, and her notes to him*

# E.F. Gebhardt:
# Factotum
# and Confidant

The day is perfect — just above zero,
perfectly still and a fair covering of snow
in most places, but sleighing not good in
all directions...
> — memo from Gebhardt to Lila Webb

Seeing to the care of her gardens when
Lila was away, as he had seen to Teddy
Roosevelt's speedy rendezvous with a wait-
ing train in 1901 when McKinley was shot,
and seen to the smoothness of Frederica's
wedding logistics in 1905, was E.F.
Gebhardt, the Webbs' factotum. Every large
estate needed a reliable, intelligent, loyal
man to watch over everything when the
owners were away. At Shelburne Farms, E.F.
Gebhardt functioned well in this role from
the turn of the century up into the 1920s.

Exactly where Gebhardt acquired his
range of skills — besides managing the
house and gardens, he seemed equally at
home as accountant, engineer, social arbiter,

confidant and memo writer extraordinaire —or how he gained the Webbs' confidence, is not known. But in 1902, the year Dr. Webb made a run for the Republican nomination for governor of Vermont, Gebhardt encouraged Lila to tell her husband that he had to compete more aggressively against his rival, Fletcher Proctor. The factotum risked rebuttal when he suggested the doctor's character was too aloof and restrained. The old-fashioned attitude that competition undermined his dignity was a fine sentiment, Gebhardt agreed, but not one that would put Dr. Webb in Montpelier. Eventually, the aspirant withdrew from the race.

Gebhardt managed the house and the gardens on an annual allowance. Apparently, when Woodgate was away from the residence with the Webbs, Gebhardt interviewed and hired needed staff. He kept the accounts. He negotiated with local suppliers and contractors, analyzed alternatives to costly projects, such as a proposed new refrigeration system Dr. Webb liked and he didn't, and later on, after the doctor's health began to fail, explained how some of the new mechanical devices functioned so Lila could make a better decision whether to buy or make do with the old.

Through the years the memorandums Gebhardt wrote varied from blunt directives to personal letters couched as business correspondence. Written first in longhand, then typed in duplicate, they report such diverse matters as the questionable payment of guests' chauffeurs (Gebhardt paid them), the right way to handle a hospital's request for a sizeable contribution (Lila granted the fund raisers an audience), the circumstances of young Van's goods left carelessly out in the rain at the depot (they weren't, he reported), the way to soften an old employee's dying (he brought in a nurse who did "more real good in two hours last Sunday morning than all the doctors that have been in attendance."), and the veritable revolving door of upholstering and maintenance questions (he usually did what Lila asked, although sometimes he didn't) that went with keeping the house attractive and up-to-date.

Lila writes to him on stationery, from New York, from Maine, from Paris. His replies often crackle with dry humor. He is always polite, defers to her judgment, and then introduces his own as something she may want to consider.

As Shelburne Farms leaves behind the glitter and prosperity of the Gilded Era, and must adapt and deal with the start of Modern Times, grimly heralded by the carnage of World War I in Europe, it becomes apparent that the Webbs are still very wealthy but priorities need to be established. Their resources cannot sustain an agricultural estate as grand as once envisioned. The question of what is to receive priority attention in and about the house seems to have gradually become Lila's responsibility to decide, and Gebhardt's to administer.

A particularly well documented time, during which many memos and letters were exchanged, was the two-year period, 1916-1917. Dr. Webb's health was poor and he was confined to a wheelchair, placing more decision-making burdens on Lila. Her gardens had been completed the year before, and major redecorating work was now underway in the house. Allusions to some of the ripple effects of World War I, which raged in Europe but had not yet drawn America in, are present in the correspondence. But mostly it focuses on the Big House, its functioning, and the daily challenges of keeping everything going.

In January Gebhardt writes Lila about her preference for cream colored floor tiles in a new bathroom. China white fixtures, which she wants, go well with a China white floor, he says, but does China white compliment cream? He thinks not. As the floor will go in the bathroom servicing the golf locker room, Gebhardt suggests silver grey tiles, a color popular in public places. "I feel sure you will not like this cream sample," he writes, "but I may be wrong."

The following month Lila tells him to

please make sure Dr. Webb's clothes have been removed from his bedroom, which is being worked on; the doctor is worried about his things.

In March, while taking a walk in the vicinity of the greenhouses, Lila comes across a collection of rubbish outside the house of one of the Farms' staff. Immediately taking up her pen when back in the Big House, she writes to Gebhardt, "Quite disgraceful. Papers strewn around a place have such an untidy appearance. I always ask all my golf guests to please try and remember to put the tissue wrapping from their balls in their pockets or togs, and not throw them on the links." Could he see to this matter immediately?

During the second week of April, a lively exchange takes place in regard to the wallpapering of the Pink Room. The paper hanger has made the point to Gebhardt, which he thinks is worthy of passing along, that the angles of the wallpaper she sent butt together all wrong. Seeing his point, Lila wires from New York that she is shipping another style of wallpaper for the room.

In May, spring's allure in the air, the question of a young chauffeur taking the maids into Burlington on their day off draws the following broadside from the factotum: "I believe in 'Safety First' in these matters." Alternative means of transport are arranged for the girls to visit the city.

Also in May painters prove hard to come by. Referring to work planned for the Orchard Cottage, located a half mile up the lakeshore from the Big House, Gebhardt writes his boss, "With four painters this job could probably be done in about three weeks (allowing for some bad weather) but I haven't the four painters, or the three weeks."

In August, he apologizes for disobeying an order. "This seems to be my mistake," he admits after cutting down an old and deformed apple tree. In a rare fumbling of syntax, he writes, "I should of course not have done this if I had not been under [the] impression that you did not care."

Memos detail the progress of work in Lila's Overlook. Descriptions for the mixing of paints read like lead-championing cookbooks.

In the spring of 1917 a memo from Gebhardt suggests that the Farms are falling behind the times. He says the implements are old and that five or six horses are so decrepit the town listers are not even appraising them for taxes. He thinks it may be time they traded the nags in for one of those newfangled tractors. Previously lukewarm to these machines, he has decided the bugs have been ironed out. For $915 a new tractor can be bought. It would replace two teams of horses.

The tractor purchase is approved.

Shortly thereafter, an interesting development threatens tradition in the kitchen. Gebhardt calculates how much electricity is required to power a new Westinghouse range, and somewhat sadly reports that the extant power plant is inadequate for the job. Storage from the plant keeps three hundred and fifty lights glowing for one hour, he notes. A new range, with both griddles and the oven cooking three meals a day, requires the equivalent of seven hundred and fifty hours of house lights, double the plant's capacity. Despite this, he thinks one of these new ranges is a purchase Lila should consider. He writes, "When one without a cook or maid can prepare the oven at night, set the clock, and find breakfast all prepared in the morning," why not buy one?

Lila doesn't. Maybe her cook liked coal.

# After the Heyday: The 1920s

For Shelburne Farms the 1920s marked the start of a long decline. So promising of great things in the 1890s, this pace-setter in agricultural experimentation and breeding seemed to come to a standstill after the first decade of the new century. Farmers bought cars and tractors, not hackneys, so that venture failed. The agricultural divisions of the Farms generated little if any profit, yet they continued to operate. Cash flowed out in support of the estate, the Adirondack game park Nehasane, and a new winter place in Florida. The doctor's health continued to decline, and Lila, assuming more control of the Farms' decision-making, lacked any training whatsoever in business.

As for outside interests, Dr. Webb's Wagner Palace Car Company, which forty years previously had earmarked the young man for railroad empire stardom, had ended up in the hands of George Pullman. Related railroad ventures had suffered similar fates in a climate of fierce, protracted competition. Recently legislated income

taxes, and increasing property taxes, added to the cash problems. That the Farms continued running as efficiently as they had was due in large part to Gebhardt and the supervisors, most of whom had worked for the Webbs for years. These same individuals may have also kept the Farms from specializing in dairy, a change most smaller operations in Vermont had made to survive, and thus by perpetuating an outdated agricultural style, insured that the Farms they saved also never prospered.

To the outside world few visible signs yet revealed these weakening internal dynamics. Relatively, the Webbs were still wealthy, prominent and powerful. Visitors to Shelburne Farms saw an estate almost as busy, formidable and as grand as ever. But, as with many of their Gilded Age contemporaries, the boundless potential the Webbs had held in their hands prior to the 20th century had slipped away. That brief and wondrous time, when man seemed on the threshold of a dream, a dream in which science wedded industry and all mankind benefitted, was left behind along with the dusty broughams and the deserted servants' quarters. World War I and the advent of Modernism made that era seem distant and almost quaint by comparison. Idealistic, singleminded pursuits of landscape and empire dreams, free from political intervention, were not to be seen again.

## Three Visitors: A Local Boy, A Teamster's Daughter, and A Society Relative

Truman Webster, who lived in Shelburne, first visited the Farms in 1922, when he accompanied his brother David to the Pheasantry. Dr. Webb met them there and exchanged arcane insights and observations on the breeding of birds with David, who at age eighteen was an avid ornithologist. Eventually, the doctor gave David several birds, including a pair of Canada geese.

Truman recalls Dr. Webb as an imposing figure erect in a wheelchair, dressed in tweeds, his secretary by his side. A full-time game keeper looked after the geese, English pheasants, quail and other birds. The chauffeur and valet were nearby, usually leaning on the fender of the Cadillac limousine, the Brewster green one with the bulge in the roof to accommodate the doctor's stovepipe hat. With his high-pitched voice, white hair

and two Scotties running around the wheelchair and leaping into his lap, Dr. Webb was a memorable figure to a young visitor.

Accompanying David to the Webbs' for lunch one day, Truman remembers the tall, imposing Mr. Woodgate greeting them in the Main Hall. The steward led the nervous twosome down a long corridor redolent with flowers and they joined about twenty-five other guests in the Marble Room. Truman could hear the splashing of water. The Conservatory was dense with ferns and palms. There was a fountain. A bower of orchids arched over it. Four liveried footmen, wearing gloves, served lunch from marble tables whose legs were carved with animals. Dr. Webb never appeared. Truman learned later that he took his meals in his own quarters on the second floor.

After lunch, Lila held court on the terrace in front of the Marble Room. She wore a white dress and a large hat that shaded her face. Mr. Gebhardt, upon her instructions, strolled down into the gardens and invited visitors she had recognized up to the terrace for tea or a cocktail. It was late July, the height of the lily season, and the gardens were open to the public. A slight breeze from the lake made the tall crowns of the elms sway. The ladies, their husbands behind, crossed the lawn, holding their hats on with a free hand. As they greeted Madam

Webb, as Truman called her, Lila smiled and concentrated on their lips before responding. For by then Lila Webb, who had had a hearing problem for much of her life, was practically deaf.

A story Truman heard later reveals a different side of the gracious lady. Once when she missed the train to New York she decided she could catch it at the next stop south, in Vergennes. As Alec Cain, her chauffeur, raced the train to Vergennes, Lila crouched on the floor because the potholes in the dirt road threw her repeatedly against the limousine's roof.

A quite different perspective on the Webbs and the Big House during the 1920s comes from Ellen St. George, the daughter of a teamster who went to work at the Farms in 1917, when Ellen was five.

Ellen lived in a Farms cottage, went to school in the town of Shelburne with twenty-five other estate children, and remembers twenty or so teams of horses going out daily into the fields. "O goodness gracious, there was an awful string of them used to go out," she recalls fondly.

She remembers Dr. Webb traveling the grounds in his buggy, Scotties along for the ride. He wanted things neat and shipshape, the cottages and houses hidden from view by cedars. Restricted to the buggy the old man seemed removed and aloof to a young girl, and sounded gruff and impatient when ordering the help about. After an active life, a sedentary old age obviously disagreed with the doctor.

Ellen's father drew coal to the Big House during the winter, and cut ice for the Ice House. He was also one of the dairymen and had to make sweet-cream butter for the doctor. Her father told her that Dr. Webb insisted on fresh eggs as well, and would only eat those stamped fresh that particular morning. He had a refrigerator up in his area of the house and ate most of his meals there in the company of his valet.

A large staff still ran the house then — parlormaids, chambermaids, butlers — all under Walter Woodgate. In 1925, Ellen's mother went to work for him as second cook. This job entailed helping the English cook with meals and feeding the staff.

Everything in the kitchen was prepared from scratch. The cook took the daily menu to Lila in the morning. She reviewed it. "Very rare she would disturb the menu," Ellen says. "How gracious a person she was. She'd open her house up to fifty or sixty people that she would never see. They could have anything they wanted."

Vegetables were carted up from the gardens and greenhouses for the cook to choose from. Ellen's mother helped dress lots of game and fowl. She assisted with the prepa-

ration of puddings, pastries and meats. Black bean soup was popular, sieved and layered with sliced hard-boiled eggs. The cook worked until 3:00 in the afternoon, then was off for an hour. The janitor cleaned and rekindled the coal stove at 4:00, getting it red hot. "She was fussy about it, too," Ellen says about that stove.

At dinnertime the food was carried, piping hot, into the Butler's Pantry from where two butlers served it in the dining room. Leftovers went to the staff the following noon for their lunch in the adjacent servants' dining room.

All these meals, and the boarding of guests, and the clothing of family and servants resulted in large piles of laundry, Ellen says. She saw the sizeable system that handled all this wash functioning at full steam.

Laundresses, who were older women compared to the maids, worked in a two-story building a short distance from the house. These women tended big coalstoves on which sat large tubs filled with boiling water. They peeled soap shavings into the steaming water, then dumped in the wash. They stirred the laundry about with wooden sticks, then lifted the items out, dripping, carrying them on the sticks to large soapstone rinse basins. Clothing, sheets, napkins—everything was rinsed repeatedly, until all soap residue was gone. A man

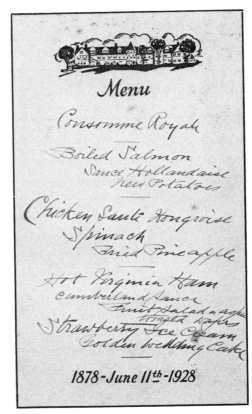

*Menu from a fiftieth wedding anniversary celebration at the house, June 11, 1928.*

servant lugged dripping baskets heaped with wet linen and sheets and clothes out to a latticed drying area. There, the women hung them with clothespins.

Ironing, which took place on the second floor, was a time consuming job. The women working there might have fifty sheets to do if the house was filled with guests. Napkins were ironed so the Webb coat-of-arms, an eagle with a crown, was displayed prominently. "They mangled their linen," Ellen says, referring to the machine with rollers used to smooth and press linen and sheets.

Once they were ready to be returned to the house, the parlormaids carried the loads of linen, clothes and sheets in baskets, and distributed them to their respective closets and bureaus on the different floors.

Another frequent visitor during these years was Lila's niece, Sheila Burden Lawrence, the daughter of Adele Florence (Sloan), the diarist. On Sundays, when visiting, Sheila played golf with Lila, then joined other guests for the traditional terrace luncheon. As a hostess, Lila was always enchanting, Sheila claims, always easy to get along with.

A party Sheila remembers well occurred on July 4, 1992, when about twenty mostly young people descended on the Big House. The weather was beautiful. Each couple was given a buggy, a horse, a caddy and a canoe. "You can imagine the time we had," she laughs, recalling romantic trots on the macadamed roads and competitive golf matches on the Shelburne Golf Links.

"There was always fun," she claims. "The people were fun, and the place was attrac-

tive. It was never stiff."

Aunt Lila gave her gifts: a bed, a desk. When engaged, Sheila and her fiancé came and stayed in the house. Lila told her in the morning to go out under the porte-cochère where there was an engagement present for her. "So I hustled out," Sheila says. "And there was the most beautiful station wagon, a brand new Ford station wagon."

Yet, despite the gaiety, Lila was having a trying time as the doctor's health slipped away, Sheila realized. On the occasions she visited, she saw the doctor only once. Lila stayed in the public's eye regardless, and retained a sense of graciousness and hospitality reminiscent of the Gilded Age. She worked in her gardens, played golf, traveled. She continued to live a full and varied life despite her deafness and diminishing resources, while the doctor stayed more and more in his quarters, becoming in his last years a virtual recluse.

Dr. Webb died in the Big House in the early fall of 1926. A simple funeral service took place in the Main Hall, which was darkened with blue curtains andd lit by candles in silver candalabra.

The following year an early frost claimed the bay trees and the English boxwood pyramids, and Lila's gardens began their decline. Finances necessitated a reduction

in garden staff. By 1930 the gardens that had stretched alongside the lake as a visual counterpoint to the house were shrinking, with plantings discontinued and some terraces reverting to lawn. Winter frost heaved brick walls. Efforts by Lila to save her gardens focused on new directions requiring less labor and maintenance.

By 1933, seven years after Dr. Webb's death, the house also began to show signs of neglect. The Library, Main Hall and Game Room remained as before, but extra bedrooms on the upper floors suffered from lack of attention. Woodgate still greeted guests at the door, and Lila held court on the terrace on Sunday afternoons. Soon the sound of a fountain no longer graced lunches in the Marble Room, the Conservatory having been removed and the wall bricked up.

# The Middle Years: 1936-1956

After Lila's death in 1936, Vanderbilt Webb, who as a boy had taken "bully" good rides across the meadows and stalked dejectedly off the golf links after playing poorly with Woodgate, assumed the position of master of Shelburne Farms. His older brother, Seward, inherited Nehasane in the Adirondacks. Frederica inherited the hook of land her grandfather, Dr. Webb, had coveted and then bought half a century before, Shelburne Point. James Watson, the eldest brother, already owned Southern Acres, the southernmost part of the estate, it having been given to him by Dr. Webb as a wedding gift in 1910.

Therefore, the estate remained relatively intact after the deaths of the founding generation. It still included over two thousand acres of land and all the major buildings except the Breeding Barn, which was located on Southern Acres.

It also required considerable maintenance and subsidies. The buildings were aging and the Farms losing money. The task of sustaining the estate, given the sub-division of family wealth and the increasing taxes, became an even greater burden than before. A lawyer from New York, even a good one like Vanderbilt Webb, with substantial wealth and a dynamic wife, could not afford continuing annual deficits from an outmoded farm nor could he pay the salaries of too many liveried footmen, presuming such relics could be found during the Depression. In a way, Vanderbilt Webb inherited an agricultural dinosaur that had, so far, refused to succumb to the violent changes in economic weather.

In this situation he had plenty of company. Throughout the Northeast, second- and third-generation owners of estates were wondering what to do with them. Taxes increased. Maintenance costs escalated. Some heirs had long ago lost faith in their parents' ideals. Others were broke. Still others wanted mobility more than they cared for mansions. To most of them, the responsibility for the extended family an estate necessitated must have seemed ludicrous in an age of bread lines.

Consequently, estate sales and sub-divisions became almost common.

In this atmosphere Van Webb's approach to estate ownership was an anachronism. Retaining a manager for the Farms, he lived eleven months out of the year in New York. During the summer season his wife, Aileen, opened the Big House and stayed there with the four children, Derick, William, Barbara and Richard. On long weekends and during his month vacation, Van joined them.

During the other months a caretaker occupied a room, and watched over sheeted furniture and empty corridors.

Just what the fate of Shelburne Farms might have been under Van Webb's management — if he had elected to forsake law, as his        father had forsaken medicine — seems worth speculating about, for of all the doctor's children he was the one who had lived there the most and who seemed to have inherited his mother's love of the place. An unassuming and modest man, Van Webb's business abilities impressed those he dealt with. He prided himself in eliminating waste and in getting to the heart of a problem. Labeled "the brains of that outfit" by one astute observer, this New York lawyer had savvy and a track record of success in challenging projects, including a long involvement with the restoration of Colonial Williamsburg. Given this background, certainly Van Webb had the potential to turn Shelburne Farms around. And yet possibly a sentimental attachment to the past, to the era of polo in the Breeding Barn, orchids in the Conservatory, and golf out the side door, made the severe changes necessary — specialization, mechanization, termination of farm staff not contributing to profits, and many others — too hard for him to contemplate. Undoubtedly, he recognized that a streamlined, modern Farms meant a ruthless elimination of the old, and he knew himself well enough to admit he was the wrong man for it. At any rate, he kept the Farms operational, in lieu of a number of lesser alternatives, and life in the Big House continued — if not as grand nor for as extended periods as before — festive, fun and eventful.

Van's brother, Seward, a sportsman who boxed (he once entertained world heavyweight champion Gene Tunney at the Big House; the champ liked to crack the busted bones in his nose for a laugh at dinner) and

raced cars, decided Nehasane paled in comparison to the Big House as a summer place, and in 1938 moved his family back across the lake and into the house, too. To accommodate both families, the brothers divided the mansion: the Van Webbs in the older, original wing, using the Tea Room for dining, the Main Hall and Library for entertaining, and the South Porch for enjoying the sunsets; the Seward Webbs eating and socializing in the Marble Room, relaxing in the Game Room, and occupying the North Porch and the bedrooms of the Westerly Extension. Given the size of the house, this arrangement worked fine, at least for a few summers, until the Seward Webbs moved their vacation home downeast, to Bar Harbor.

At this time, in the late 1930s, the servants' wing no longer functioned. Van called in contractors for salvage estimates, but delayed demolition because of the expense. He built a modern kitchen closer to the dining rooms, in what had been the Butler's Pantry. Staff brought north each summer consisted of Arthur Harris, a butler who had learned the trade under the venerable Woodgate, and Agnes Murphy, their private maid, cook and housekeeper. A cook's helper and four part-time maids were hired locally to help with the meals and cleaning.

The gardens were under Aileen Webb's

supervision and she implemented plans to slow their deterioration. As the English cottage style was no longer in vogue, she reverted the plantings to an earlier Victorian formality, much reduced in size. Darcy Patterson, who would oversee the gardens for many decades, assumed the responsibilities of head gardener.

Numerous guests came and went. Both the Van Webbs and the Seward Webbs entertained and lived informally. The variety of sport and pleasure offerings decreased. Guests continued to sail, and to play tennis and squash, but gas rationing during World War II meant no fuel for mowing fairways and greens, so Shelburne Golf Links soon reverted to meadow. It was a far cry from the days of caddies shouting, "Fore!" or Mr. Woodgate shaking his head as the young Van stalked off towards home after missing a three-foot putt.

One popular new pastime did emerge during the war years though; Van Webb, his wife Aileen, and their guests, liked to help with the haying. Only one team of horses remained then — the others had all been replaced with tractors — and the team's hay wagon and ambience proved magnetic. Buttoning the cuffs of their sleeves, the Webbs and their guests joined the farm hands in the meadows, and tossed bales. At 4:00 in the afternoon both animals and tractors stopped working. John Boisvert, a man still employed at the estate in 1986, brought out tea and sandwiches. When hauled in at twilight, the hay was stored to feed milk cows in the now predominantly dairy operation.

World War II's effects on the house, if not as immediately noticeable as the potholes in the roads and the waving grass covering the fairways, were substantial. The removal of the coal furnace from the cellar, its steel bound for re-smelting into bullets and armor, proved most detrimental. This 19th-century behemoth once consumed a coal car of fuel in a single day, or so it was said, and dismantling required the services of the Shelburne Volunteer Fire Department for the better part of a month. Subsequently, the unheated stone walls of the foundation began to shift due to frost penetration. Brick columns lost their plumb. The cement floor heaved and cracked. Up on the roof, delayed gutter work resulted in small leaks. Inside the house, in some of the rooms, paint peeled, as did wallpaper.

During the war the seawall deteriorated in places and the broad strip of lawn in front of the garden balustrade toppled into Lake Champlain. Winter frosts heaved more of the brick walls and the columns of the pergola rotted and reversed roles with the grapevines they once supported. After the war a local florist bought the greenhouses, dismantled the roofs and walls, and took them away. All that remained of what had been three acres of vegetables, flowers and exotic plants of all descriptions, was Darcy Patterson's cottage, which he was given use of for the rest of his life.

This "for life" tenancy applied to the dwellings of a number of the Webbs' long term help. Walter Woodgate, the English steward whose presence dominated the house staff from the 1890s until Lila Webb's death in 1936, was given use of his quarters in the Annex. He continued to summer there until 1958. Farm help enjoyed similar retirement privileges after decades of work. These arrangements reflect on the nature of the master/servant system, one without legal safeguards but not without a sense of moral responsibility on the part of the landowners toward certain members of their extended family.

Well into the 1950s, the Van Webbs continued to summer at the house. Their son, Derick, who had taken over management of the Farms after World War II, lived in what was called the Orchard House, a dwelling a half mile to the north.

Derick's four boys and two girls spent many hours in the Big House. Their voices echoed down the long halls. They played tag in the long-abandoned and cobwebbed servants' quarters.

One of the boys, Marshall, recalls walking from the Orchard House alongside the lake —an adventurous outing for a small lad— and over to the Big House in the morning. He sat at the foot of the bed in the room where his great-grandfather, Dr. Webb, had lived, and talked with his grandmother, Aileen, as she ate her breakfast.

By this time the matriarch of the family had a considerable reputation in American crafts. In 1939 Aileen had established the American Craftsman's Coöp Council, and two years later, started publishing *Craft Horizons* magazine. Her efforts would soon be instrumental in opening the doors of the American Craft Museum in New York.

When Marshall visited her, he was a big-eyed youngster chatting with his old grandmother, and afterwards an exuberant boy running full speed down the hallways. The vast, friendly place beckoned his feet to fly and his mind to wander. Every Sunday, after church, he stuffed himself at the family luncheon on the terrace. Roast beef, peas and strawberry shortcake, the strawberries cultivated by the then legendary Darcy Patterson, swelled his stomach. "It was heaven," he claims.

*Derick Webb in his office at the Farm Barn*

# Changing Times: 1956-1986

> Things at the Big House were always bigger than life.
> — Emily Wadhams

Van Webb died in 1956, passing the legacy of Shelburne Farms to his son Derick. Derick's attachment to the architecture was not strong. He did move his family into the Big House from his Orchard House during the summer months, but the move may have been precipitated as much by obligation as by desire. Derick's heart was in the agricultural aspects of the Farms, which he had managed for the past two decades, not in the buildings. Consequently, their maintenance remained a low priority as other needs competed for limited funds.

Derick's mother, Aileen Osborn Webb, considered staying on in the house during the summer season, but quickly found six grandchildren and their ceaseless rock-and-roll too much of a change to her well established style. The matriarch built a cottage for herself at the edge of the gardens, which she continued to oversee.

Staying on as gardener was the inimitable Darcy Patterson, now quite elderly himself and facing formidable tasks. Due to lack of attention, certain sections of the gardens were drifting back towards the natural style (Gertrude Jeckyll might have been pleased) on their own. The white columns of the pergola had long ago rotted, reversing roles with the grapevines they originally had supported. Aileen had the once grand structure torn down. To reduce costs she had scattered plantings consolidated.

Moving into the 1960s, the house and gardens assumed yet a different role; they seemed a kind of sprawling summer camp for the growing children of Derick and Elizabeth Webb, who moved the whole family over from the Orchard House every May. Quentyn, Marshall and Alec bunked in the Yellow Room. Mary stayed in the Rose Room, Lisa in the adjacent West Room, and the youngest child, Robert, called the small, semi-circular (the exterior is a turret) Tower Room his own. The children romped in the hallways, played softball on the lawn, shared large, informal dinners on the terrace with their parents and friends, and listened to Elvis, and then the Beatles, in the Game Room.

Their mother, Elizabeth, liked to give parties for her six children and their friends.

"It was really a blast," Emily Wadhams, who attended some of the events as a teenager, remembers.

Buffet-style meals were served. Kids played pool and ping pong. They chased each other around the gardens and explored every room and cranny in the house. Sometimes late at night they snuck into the servants' wing with a flashlight to scare themselves. They danced and swam and had a good time.

Then in the late 1960s, as this generation approached adulthood, their father, Derick, found himself forced to accept what had long been in the making. In a difficult but foresighted move, he called the family together and explained that increasing taxes, dwindling resources and escalating farm deficits threatened the future of the Farms. The facts, unfortunately, pointed towards liquidation. Derick remained open to alternatives, however, and encouraged input from his children, the oldest of whom was in his early 20s.

"He made it a family problem," Alec Webb, then in his teens, recalls.

Marshall Webb remembers being bowled over. Not until college had he realized what Shelburne Farms represented. His family owned what Americans in the vanguard of the environmental movement were starting to talk about: a powerful landscape and irreplaceable buildings, natural resources with aesthetic, cultural and historical resonance. Taking a stand to save them would be taking a stand for the environment.

With no real plan, but with unanimous intent, the children decided to attempt to save the estate from changing hands or being broken up into real estate gems. They told their father they would all stick right here and work on this — as long as he did not sell the place.

Derick, who after all had spent his life working towards the same goal, was skeptical. So were family advisors and lawyers. But idealism, that abstract buttress of the 1960s, prevailed.

With Derick's guidance and cooperation, plans were devised by the young Webbs to evolve Shelburne Farms once again into an innovative agricultural enterprise that was similar in spirit but different in its operations from the estate Dr. Webb had created almost a century before. Accordingly, in 1972, Shelburne Farms Resources, a non-profit company with cultural and educational divisions, was formed. Initial projects included a summer camp for disadvantaged children, farmers markets and a craft cooperative. Over the next few years, Marshall Webb became the forester and woodlot manager for Shelburne Farms Resources, Alec Webb the general manager, and Marilyn Webb, Alec's wife, the president. Derick Webb, whose foresight had initiated the changes to keep the Farms alive, would in 1984 bequeath his property and the buildings to the non-profit operation managed by his children and steered by a board of directors.

The first years of this reorganized Shelburne Farms proved tenuous and challenging. No railroad fortune guaranteed the future as it had for Dr. Webb in 1886. Having forfeited their inheritance and forsaken alternative occupations, the young Webbs found themselves in a go-for-broke position. Many people told them they would never pull the whole thing off. Some days, Marshall admits, he got a little overwhelmed by the scope of what they were trying to do. It seemed a little crazy. Also rather romantic. But they believed in what they were doing, sought input and expert advice on all major conservation issues and business questions, and stuck to their goals.

During this time, just where the Big House would fit in the future of a revitalized Shelburne Farms remained a question. In 1974 it was still the summer residence of the Derick Webbs. But then, when Derick and his wife, Elizabeth, were divorced and the continuity of family occupancy disrupted, circumstances seemed appropriate for a timely transition from private use to public,

*Mozart Festival concert, 1984*

a transition that would guarantee the house its rightful place in future plans. An alternative cultural use was found and that very summer a hundred classical-music fans came to the Marble Room to enjoy the first Mozart Festival concert conducted in the house. Subsequent concerts drew increasingly larger crowds. The concerts fit naturally into the house and promised to generate revenue for much needed maintenance — the lack of which continued its discreet attack on the roof, foundation and interior — without compromising either the authenticity of the building or the past uses.

The following summer, in 1975, in a bemusing reversal of roles, Marshall Webb

and his wife, the Emily Wadhams who had had fun there as a teenager, moved into the house as staff. Working for Shelburne Farms Resources, Emily was officially the Big House director and Marshall the maintenance man.

"I remember walking through those front doors and getting hit by the old, musty smell of the place," Emily says. For her the house radiated a powerful physical presence. Afternoon light seemed almost tangible, an elixir of magic.

The couple managed the series of concerts and hosted the first paying guests, a group of teachers attending a ten day workshop. Emily maintained the tradition of fresh flowers in the Main Hall, the Marble Room and in the bedrooms that were occupied. The flowers came from the gardens where Aileen Osborn Webb, now in her eighties, maneuvered about the terraces with a walker. Below the main flower beds the rose garden still bloomed. The balustrade still overlooked the lake. Semi-circular beds of annuals lent color and spirit to the plantings, which were much reduced in size and obviously deteriorating in quality.

In 1976, Marshall and Emily offered rooms to guests, boarded between twenty and twenty-five musicians who participated in that summer's Mozart Festival, and operated the concerts. Both remember the time fondly. In a way the Big House had come full circle, back to the multiple roles originally envisioned: resort hotel, business headquarters (albeit a small one), figurative hub for the new Shelburne Farms, and dormitory for twenty or more, depending on how many musicians were present. The one role missing was that of family residence. And, of course, a few other things had changed. Such as the fourth-generation Webbs now making the beds and serving the meals. Emily and Marshall also figured bills and inserted screens in windows. And, indicative of pressing repair problems, placed rain buckets strategically in the hallways at the first rumble of a summer thun-

der shower echoing across the lake. As for the ambience of the house, well, concerts on the South Porch at sunset followed by dancing in the Marble Room late into the night must have evoked their share of Great Gatsby fantasies in both the musicians and the house guests.

Once Marshall and Emily ended their tenure in the late 1970s, house directors were hired for subsequent summer seasons. Into the 1980s the concerts continued, along with workshops taught by the musicians. Guests were boarded and fed. And small business groups often held seminars.

These varied uses of the house did not address the continuing deterioration however, and problems in the cellar and on the roof had reached the point where, to be repaired properly, they demanded large expenditures of cash. Even these major problems, if taken care of, promised no long-term solution to the Queen Anne mansion's age, which was showing. The time had clearly arrived for a thorough and complete restoration; otherwise, annual repairs and patchwork would both drain cash reserves and eventually erode sympathy — a crucial ingredient of any sizeable restoration — towards the house.

Analyzing this dilemma, the Webbs and the board of directors recognized a fundamental truth: that during the early

1980s, as more of the general public had enjoyed the programs and events at the house and the Farms, it had become obvious that many of these visitors wanted to see the buildings almost as much as they wanted to know about farming or conservation or listen to music. Architecture on such a scale lured people's eyes and primed their imaginations.

In light of this realization, and given the history and recent uses of the house, the board of directors decided that turning it into an inn seemed a natural evolution. In 1983 they voted to go ahead with the transformation.

Such a transformation promised foremost to maintain the architectural authenticity of the house and to keep it a social testament of America's Gilded Age. It also promised to open the residence up for the public's enjoyment, to provide additional revenue for the support of other programs, and to fulfill part of the revitalized Farms mission, which was "to maintain and adapt its historic buildings and landscape for teaching and demonstrating the stewardship of natural and agricultural resources." As a place to eat and stay, an inn would offer a taste of the good country life as lived by the W. Seward Webb during America's era of boundless dreams, the Gilded Age.

# Becoming An Inn

One thing I'm doing all my spare time is trying to find a key for every room in that house. I've got about a thousand keys. I'd sit down by a door and I'd try about two hundred keys, and so far I've found only about fifteen.

— John Boisvert,
lifelong employee of the Farms

During the intermission of a Mozart Festival concert, architect Martin Tierney took a stroll with his wife out on the broad lawns of the house. Looking back at the crowd and the South Porch, he remarked dreamily, "If I ever had a sabbatical, I'd love to live here for six weeks and do a complete set of drawings."

Three weeks later his phone rang. It was Marilyn Webb, president of Shelburne Farms. She wanted to talk to him about restoration of the Big House and transformation of the residence into an inn.

"It was like an act of God," Martin said.

Soon, as project architect, he frightened bats in the attic and dodged streamers of pipe insulation dangling in the cellar. He went up on the roof to examine decades of patch jobs and busted gutters. He inspected the long-derelict servants' wing. Basically, he concluded, the main house was sound and the servants' wing in bad shape. Several problems demanded immediate attention though. The ruined gutter system, which had funneled water away from the house, now funneled it into the cellar; a heaved cement floor and accelerated foundation damage were the consequences. The slate roof, with its numerous ridges, valleys, chimneys and dormers, needed competent repair, not further patching; small leaks were on the verge of becoming expensive headaches. In addition, the thirteen clustered chimneys required repointing as some of the mortar had fallen out. Otherwise, most of the restoration work, albeit extensive, seemed straightforward: replacing rotted cornices, mending exterior woodwork with an epoxy system, painting, glazing windows, re-plastering interior walls and ceilings, sanding floors, and the myriad other smaller jobs a restoration of this size entailed.

*Staging surrounds a tall clustered chimney and supports two masons who are repointing the brick.*

Determining the exact layout from that heyday proved a challenge for Martin Tierney, as the original architect, Robert H. Robertson, had often neglected to date his drawings. Eventually, Martin located the 1899 floor plan in the Shelburne Farms archives. It revealed what he had suspected all along: few interior alterations had ever been undertaken. Van Webb had relocated the kitchen. And the Conservatory had been bricked up. But except for lots of peeling wallpaper, chipped paint and loose plaster, the inside of the house looked much as it had eighty years before.

Ultimately, the major obstacle to the transformation became not so much the house itself, but rather the standards for public safety that contemporary laws mandated. For the Big House, when the inspectors examined it, had all the old safety flaws: a wooden frame, numerous doors and windows, long hallways and substantial distances to exits. The inspectors all shook their heads and images of ugly partitions, sheetrocked walls, metal-core doors and a sprinkler system filled Martin's imagination.

In an effort to retain the authenticity, he arranged a luncheon for ten of the inspectors at the house. In front of these basically suspicious men, he spread seven-foot milar drawings across the marble-topped serving tables. He talked about architecture not as materials but as place, as a particular place — here, in this house, where the Webb family had lived for nearly a hundred years. With enthusiasm and description, Martin evoked some of the drama that had transpired in the rooms, in the servants' wing, on the grounds. Then he took the inspectors on a tour. He showed them around. They were affected by the place.

Vermont's B.O.C.A. basic building code, section 516.0 states that, "The provisions of this code relating to the . . . restoration . . . of buildings or structures shall not be mandatory [if such buildings are] identified and classified by the state or local government authority as historic buildings . . ." Thus, the state gave certain discretionary powers to inspectors facing unusual situations, such as the transformation of the state's largest house into an inn. The inspectors, to their credit, realized that some of the standards that served safety in more conventional situations also negated authenticity in the Big House. The end result for the public, if codes were rigidly applied, would be a much diminished cultural experience.

So these inspectors worked with Martin Tierney, and although no compromises were made regarding public safety, more aesthetically pleasing means to the same ends were found. For instance, high technology fire stops — sandwiches of sheet glass and tumescent gel that expands and forms a heat barrier at high temperatures — were selected as partitions in the corridors, meeting standards but not ruining those long suggestive views. Fire extinguishers, smoke alarms and a fire management administrator (a night watchman) sufficed as an alternative to the intrusive over-head sprinklers system.

Restoration commenced in 1985. Mark Neagley, a contractor noted for the high quality of his restoration work, was hired to supervise the project, with the emphasis on good craftsmen and the best materials in order to recapture the look and feel of the house during its late Gilded Age heyday. Yet, from the start, the size of the house, its historic significance, and the planned public occupancy complicated things. As did the servants' quarters. The wing that had once housed the thirty-odd servants who had made the combination home, resort hotel and business headquarters run smoothly had become a preservation liability. Returning the wing to some semblance of its original shape, it was estimated, would be so costly that it would jeopardize the larger task of transforming the Big House into an inn. At the same time, if the wing was razed, would the Big House still be a testament of authentic country living from the era of maid, liveried footmen, and

*At dawn, dew made the roofing slates thick, but by mid day, the hot sun often made them too hot to touch without gloves. Here Les Gove eyes a black Munson slate before cutting it.*

gamekeepers?

The quarters had been unoccupied and unheated for decades. The roof leaked. Structurally, the wing was in much worse shape than the rest of the house. The former larder for instance, looked ready to implode. Its floor had collapsed. Joist ends looked like fibrous jam. Nevertheless, the Vermont Department of Historic Preservation, which had to okay any demolition, determined the wing should be saved. How could visitors understand the workings of the Big House as a statement about the Victorian era without the part of the statement that had made everything function, asked Eric Gilbertson, director of the Department of Historic Preservation.

It was a good question. Shelburne Farms found itself caught in a dilemma: how to allocate scarce financial resources to conserve its principal historic structures and 1,000 acre property while maintaining appropriate historic authenticity.

But a compromise was reached. With the aid of an old photograph from the collection of J. Watson Webb, Jr., Martin Tierney deduced that the servants' quarters had originally been smaller, and he convinced Gilbertson and the Vermont Department of Historic Preservation that a restoration of the quarters to the earlier, and smaller, configuration would, if not exactly dupli-

cate the size of the quarters, at least retain its spirit and give visitors a suggestion of the whole. In this manner, both historical authenticity and economic reality were served, and a third of the wing was saved.

Meanwhile, restoration went forward in four overlapping stages: roof repair, structural repairs, utilities and interior work, exterior finish.

First, Brown's River Masonry erected staging to reach the clustered chimneys where bricks hung loose and bats flew in and out. Starting over the South Porch and working north, the Middlebury Slate Company replaced hundreds of broken slates (they used perfectly matching black Munson slates salvaged from the roof of the servants' quarters), flashed eyebrow windows, turret caps, and the peaks of little conical roofs. They also rebuilt the elaborate copper gutter system.

The roof work was challenging. At dawn, dew dampened the slates, making them slick. By noon, during the summer months, the slates were too hot to touch without gloves. Stagings were constantly being moved. The masons spent as much time erecting and taking down their staging as they did in repointing the thirteen chimneys. All the copper sheeting for the gutters had to be specially cut and shaped on the ground, then soldered and lugged up long

ladders. The ringing sound of slate being checked with a hammer for hardness and the plop of mud shifting from trowel to brick continued well into the fall.

Unfortunately the water damage in the basement caused by the ruined original gutter system wasn't the biggest problem down there. The streamers of pipe insulation Tierney had dodged during his initial inspection were asbestos, a carcinogenic. The asbestos had to be removed before structural repairs could begin. To do that, five workmen wearing full-face respirators and synthetic suits sealed off the contaminated area with plastic sheeting. They constructed a three-chamber entryway. Two of the chambers were changing rooms, one for work clothes and one for street clothes. The third room contained the showers. Filtered negative-pressure machines were temporarily installed to keep any airborne asbestos from somehow leaking out. Once the Big House's basement looked like a scene from a science fiction film, the asbestos was sprayed loose with water and cleaned up with shovels and vacuum cleaners. The cost was an unanticipated $50 thousand.

Compared to the asbestos headache, the installation of modern plumbing and wiring on all three floors was relatively straightforward and conventional. In the fall, crews

*Plasterer Loy Kempster repairing cracked interior ceiling.*

mentation using surviving pieces of the original nineteenth-century patterns— lambs' tongue and bellflower, egg and dart, Greek key, the fancier Roman key. First Kempster made molds of the historic pieces he wanted to replicate. Then he poured fresh plaster into his molds. The hardened ornaments were scratched on their backs and eased into place in beds of plaster.

Asked about the occasional roll a keen observer could detect in a wall, Kempster remarked, "The house is a hundred years old; it shouldn't be perfect."

To dry the plaster and keep the dozens of tradesmen warm during the cold months, four temporary gas furnaces blew hot air through a network of ducts. By March 1986 the asbestos was gone, the new gutter system kept water out of the basement, the structural work was complete, and the utilities were mostly installed. But Mark Neagley announced at a construction meeting late that month that the $1.5 million project was running away from them. It was over budget and behind schedule. "Every time you turn around," the usually calm and patient project manager said, "there's another thing to fix, another floor to shim, another wall to cut."

Marilyn Webb, Alec Webb, Marshall Webb, Martin Tierney, and future inn director Marnie Davis listened to Neagley

of electricians and plumbers started shifting from section to section of the house. Long tunnels, called chases, were cut down the hallways and into each room. Wires and pipe were laid in the chases, snaked through the walls. The hallways took on the appearance of obstacle courses, with missing squares, jutting pipes, colored wires. "The plumbers had the worst job of anyone,"

Neagley said. "They jumped through hoops fixing fixtures that hadn't been used in fifty years." Once several rooms were finished, inspectors checked them out. Then plastering, painting, and wallpapering began.

Plasterer Mike Kempster, and his wife Loy, smoothed hundreds of square yards of wall, filled dozens of holes left by the electricians and plumbers, recast original orna-

recite a list of unanticipated and expensive complications. They sat huddled in jackets and parkas around a large, sheet-draped table in the Main Hall, one of the four furnaces thrumming to one side. Workmen were lugging materials from the Tea Room through the hall and up the main stairs by the elkhead, its antlers draped with white sheets. After Neagley admitted he was no longer sure everything would be done by July 1, Marilyn Webb said she could accept the additional costs but not the delays; they had to have the inn open on time. Tierney said the inspectors, who often couldn't come and sign off on completed work as promptly as Neagley wanted them to, were overloaded. But he'd see what he could do.

Relieving the tension a little, Marnie Davis said, "We need grates for the chimneys, or all those bats are going to start coming in."

A month later, Neagley was again smiling. The bats were out, a few new sprinklers in, work back on schedule. "Overcoming all the obstacles is satisfying," he said, "a challenge to everyone's tenacity."

During the months of work, although no spicy diaries were found hidden in gutted walls, some pleasant surprises had been uncovered. When the kitchen wall was removed, for example, a fireplace was discovered, completely intact, with brass wall

*Lila Webb's office, where the steward, Walter Woodgate, once received guests. Now the reception room for the inn.*

sconces and the original woodwork. Part of the kitchen, it turned out, had once been Dr. Webb's office before a turn-of-the-century alteration .

The final stage of the restoration, exterior finish work, began in the spring. The brick facade that had replaced the original exterior of clapboards on the first floor and shingles above, back in 1903, needed extensive repointing. Wood trim and cornice work were removed and replaced. Whenever possible, materials salvaged from the servants' quarters were utilized.

Interior decorating emphasized the Gilded Ages look the Webbs had manifested in the informal, country estate style. Old

*The Louis XVI Room reproduced a style, which emphasized pastel colors and floral patterns, popular during the gilded age.*

photographs served as guides. Surviving pieces of furniture, from a Louis XVI chaise to gilt sofas to canopied beds, were returned to their turn-of-the-century locations. The Old Deerfield Fabric Company replicated some of the nineteenth-century wallpaper patterns based on surviving swaths. A few subtle changes were introduced, however. For instance, "The W. Seward Webb Room had all William Morris furnishings," house director Davis said, "so we used William Morris wallpaper. It's very masculine."

As July 1 approached, floors were sanded, hallways carpeted. People lugged furniture around cans of paint, vacuum cleaners removed dust from beneath the banisters. In one upstairs hallway, Mark Neagley calmed an irate painter whose work was getting dusty from too much action taking place all around.

At a pre-opening party, Martin Tierney smiled and looked around at the Tea Room. Craftsmen who had done the restoration work, donors who had funded it, and others were scrutinizing the bedrooms overhead, peeking into the doll houses in the third-story Play Room, listening to music in the Dining Room, strolling in the gardens, whose restoration remained an ongoing project. "It's an absolute miracle it's opening," Tierney said. "But we knew that if we really wanted it to happen, it would."

An earlier experience of one of the board of directors suggested what awaited future guests. Paul Hawken, of the Smith and Hawken Tool Company, had stayed in the Rose Room while the decision whether to restore or not restore had been debated more than a year before. Waking in the room, he had stared up at the canopy over the bed in which Frederica had slept, then glanced out the window and saw the broad lake and the alluring Adirondacks. The other way, on a book shelf, lay old novels and magazines. Everything was very still. Getting up, he went to the door, opened it and looked down the long red and velvety hallway. He felt he was in a different time and place and it was wonderful.

Guests soon agreed. That first summer, and those following, they often wrote notes, commenting on "the grandeur of life in an earlier day," on "feeling as if we were visiting another era," on the meals: grilled wild salmon served with a tarragon and chive beurre blanc, breast of goose with orange and lime sauce, roast double loin chop of Vermont lamb with rosemary sauce—to mention three specialties of Scottish chef David Taylor. And, of course, there were those who just liked being left alone so they could daydream about what it must have been like way back when. One couple from Georgia wrote, "the best part is the willing-ness to let guests do what they want as if it's a private house."

"Impeccable service—loved the after-noon teas!" added another guest, having vicariously savored a touch of the Webbs' lifestyle.

Lila Webb herself probably would have smiled at the note that read: "The formality is offset by the friendliness of the staff, which makes for an unpretentious experi-ence." Though she might have been per-plexed by the next line: "The jazz music played one morning at breakfast was great."

The Shelburne House has received two prestigious awards, the President's Historic Preservation Award for Excellence, given by the Department of the Interior and signed by President Ronald Reagan, and the Preservation Trust of Vermont Award for outstanding work in preserving state architecture.

Part of what kept the inn so authentically Victorian, of course, aside from the staff of forty-five, were the gardens. Their evolu-tion continued. For several summers brick-work continued to be redone. Then vistas along the lake shore were opened, provid-ing expansive views of the Adirondacks. An anonymous patron helped sustain the gar-den work, the intent being to retain the spirit and beauty of Lila Webb's gardens, with their architectural ornamentation,

*Looking north from Saxton's Point towards Burlington*

varied plantings, and floral design, but on a more modest scale. Peonies, irises, delphiniums, gladioli, and daisies from a cutting garden were placed in bedrooms and public rooms daily, continuing a Big House tradition.

A different time and place, a vicarious thrill, a nostalgic longing for an age when man still dreamed of controlling his own destiny—the restoration of the house at Shelburne Farms gives us all of these. And more. It ushers us into a realm where the future meets the past and where both history and tomorrow are enhanced. That makes this house both memorable and rare.

# Chronology

| | |
|---|---|
| 1880 | Dr. William Seward Webb, on railroad business for the Vanderbilt empire, visits Burlington, Vermont, for the first time. |
| 1881 | Dr. Webb, age thirty, marries Lila Vanderbilt, William Henry Vanderbilt's daughter. She is twenty-two. |
| 1882 | That summer the newlyweds rent a house in Burlington. |
| | Frederica, their first child, is born. |
| 1883 | Construction begins on Oakledge, a modest country estate on the shore of Lake Champlain in Burlington. |
| 1884 | The Webbs move into Oakledge for the summer. |
| | James Watson is born. |
| 1885 | Dr. Webb obtains options on a number of farms in Shelburne, the town south of Burlington. |
| 1886 | Acquisition of farms in Shelburne procedes in earnest. Frederick Law Olmsted, the father of American landscape architecture, tours the properties. He proposes a park-like estate alongside the lake with the house overlooking the water. |
| 1887 | Olmsted's specific recommendations arrive. His plans place the house up on Lone Tree Hill, altitude five hundred and fifteen feet, with a large park separating the house from the shore of the lake. |
| 1887-88 | A temporary residence, a Shingle Style cottage designed by architect Robert H. Robertson, is built on Saxton's Point. |
| 1889 | Aboard the *Ellesmere* and the *Marquita*, their private railroad cars, the Webbs and friends take an eighteen thousand mile journey that zigzags across the United States and includes a cruise up to Alaska. |
| | That summer, after traveling two thousand miles from Delaware with a crew of fifteen, Dr. Webb's schooner-rigged steam yacht *Elfreida* sails out onto Lake Champlain. |
| 1890 | The hub of the agricultural operations, the five-storied Farm Barn, is completed. |
| 1891 | Vanderbilt Webb is born. |
| 1893 | Shelburne Farms now comprises over three thousand acres and nearly thirty consolidated small farms. |

| | |
|---|---|
| 1894 | The New York Coaching Club takes its longest drive, a three-day trip from New York to Shelburne Farms. |
| 1895 | Construction begins on a hundred-room Queen Anne Style mansion designed by Robert H. Robertson. |
| 1899 | The house is completed. In October, Admiral Dewey, the hero of Manila, visits. |
| 1902 | Vice-president Teddy Roosevelt steamed rapidly across Lake Champlain aboard the *Elfreida* after receiving word that President McKinley has been shot. Dr. Webb makes an unsuccessful run for the Republican nomination for governor of Vermont. |
| 1903 | On New Year's Day, Vanderbilt Webb, age eleven, begins a personal diary about life on the Farms. The Coach Barn is completed. The house exterior is refaced with brick and a slate roof replaces the shingles. |
| 1905 | In a country display of New York society and wealth, Frederica, the Webb's only daughter, marries Ralph Pulitzer in Shelburne. |
| 1910 | James Watson Webb, the eldest son, is deeded Southern Acres, a sizeable portion of the estate. |
| 1912 | Lila Webb orders construction to begin on her Italian-style gardens. |
| 1914 | Two missing elements of the classical Italian-style garden, a lily pond and a balustrade are added. |
| 1917 | Shelburne Farms buys a first tractor. |
| 1918 | Red Cross nurses board at the house during World War I. |
| 1920-22 | The gardens evolve to the English cottage style. |
| 1926 | Dr. Webb dies. |
| 1927 | An early frost kills the English boxwood pyramids and bay trees in the gardens. |
| 1930-3 | The house begins a long period of genteel neglect. |
| 1936 | Lila Webb dies and her children inherit Shelburne Farms. Vanderbilt Webb and his family begin summering there. |
| 1938-40s | The Van Webb and Seward Webb families share the house during the summers. |

| | |
|---|---|
| 1941-5 | World War II changes the look of the estate. The Golf Links go to seed. Lake walls crumble. Macadamed roads, potholed and in disrepair, are torn up. In the house the furnace is removed, and cold weather begins shifting the foundation walls and the cellar floor. |
| 1946 | The three acres of greenhouses are dismantled and sold. |
| 1956 | Vanderbilt Webb dies. Derick Webb becomes the owner of Shelburne Farms. |
| 1957-67 | Derick Webb's family lives in the house during the summers. The six children enjoy the place and grounds almost as if they were at some sprawling summer camp. |
| 1969 | Economic problems threaten the existence of the estate, Derick Webb tells his family at a meeting. His children commit themselves to perpetuating Shelburne Farms as an agricultural estate. |
| 1972 | Shelburne Farms Resources, a non-profit corporation, is created. |
| 1974 | The Big House ceases to be the summer residence of the Webb family. Public use begins in July, when musicians perform the first Mozart Festival concert before a hundred fans in the Marble Room. |
| 1975-78 | The Marshall Webb family moves into the house for the summer as staff. |
| 1976 | Twenty-five musicians savor a Great Gatsby fantasy: rooming and boarding in the house and playing concerts at night. Derick Webb deeds the house to Shelburne Farms Resources. |
| 1978-83 | Summer programs and events draw the public to the house. Guests and groups are boarded and fed. |
| 1983 | A plan to restore and transform the house into an inn is approved by the board of directors. |
| 1984 | Derick Webb dies, bequeathing the remaining property and buildings to Shelburne Farms Resources. |
| 1985 | A Centennial Capital Campaign raises the money for the restoration. Work begins on the chimneys and roof. |
| 1986 | Restoration work continues. |
| 1987 | The house at Shelburne Farms becomes an inn. |

# The House At Shelburne Farms

SHELBURNE, VERMONT

## MAIN FLOOR PLAN

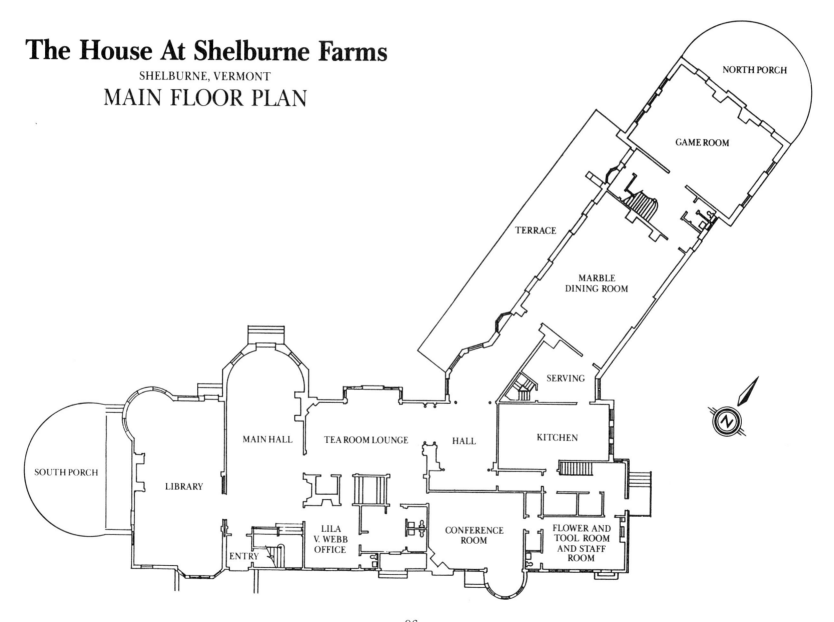

NORTH PORCH

GAME ROOM

TERRACE

MARBLE
DINING ROOM

SERVING

SOUTH PORCH

MAIN HALL

TEA ROOM LOUNGE

HALL

KITCHEN

LIBRARY

LILA
V. WEBB
OFFICE

CONFERENCE
ROOM

FLOWER AND
TOOL ROOM
AND STAFF
ROOM

ENTRY

# The House At Shelburne Farms

SHELBURNE, VERMONT

## SECOND FLOOR PLAN

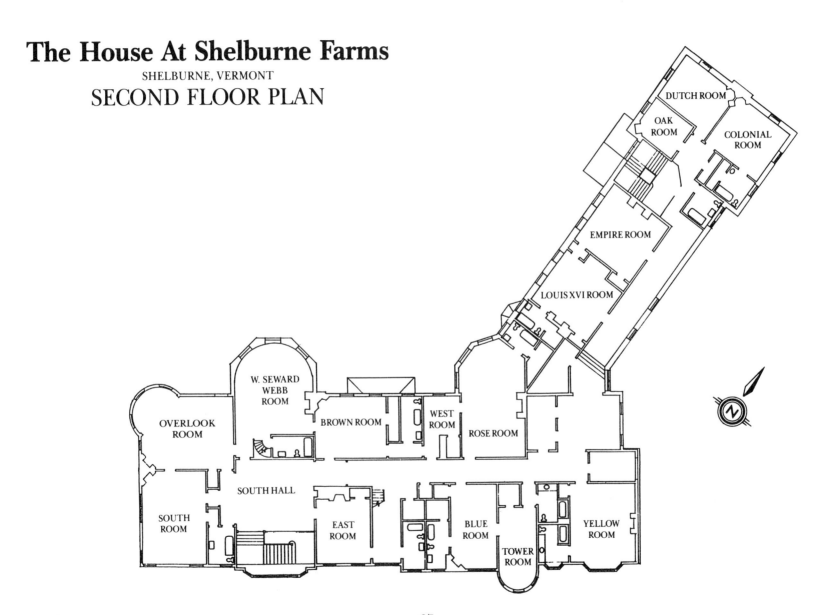

# The House At Shelburne Farms

SHELBURNE, VERMONT

## THIRD FLOOR PLAN

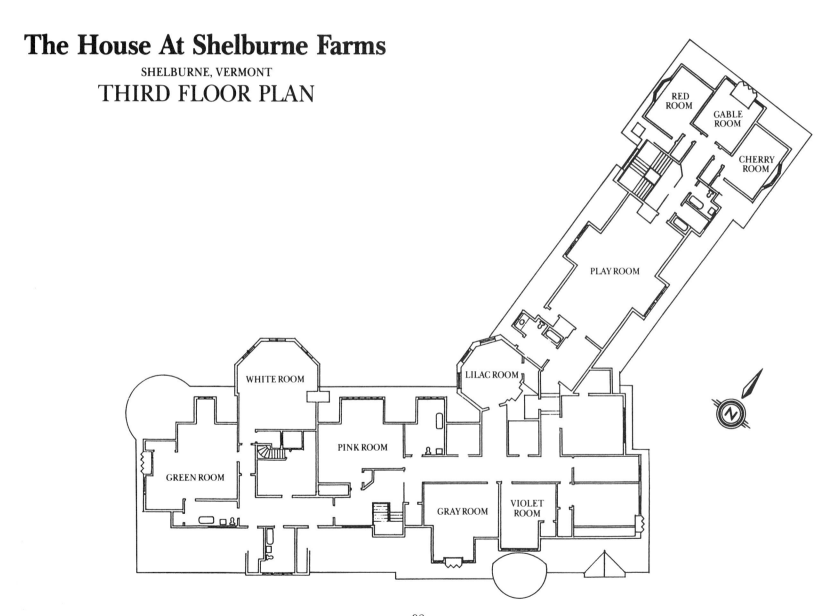

# Acknowledgements

A book of this nature is in many ways a collaborative effort, and to all those people who helped him with the work the author says, "Thank you."

In particular, he wants to express his gratitude to Marilyn Webb, then president of Shelburne Farms. Her enthusiasm and cooperation made this project possible, and her suggestions helped give it form and polish. Her staff aided the research far beyond the call of duty. Marnie Wolcott, director of the house, helped get the idea moving, and Megan Camp, director of education, guided the author through the extensive archives, answered his questions, and provided him with books and other materials that proved indispensable.

The task of writing was greatly eased by the cooperation of certain individuals and/or by the availability of their previous research and writings. To these individuals, the author is much indebted; in particular:

To the project architect, Martin Tierney, for his encouragement at the start and his knowledgeable affability throughout.

To William Lipke for sharing his considerable scholarship and wisdom, and the original research that resulted in his fine work, *Shelburne Farms: An Agricultural Estate*.

To Linda Seavy for her survey of the interior, and to Emile Mead for her monograph on the furniture and interior design.

To Del Keppelman and Susan Cady Hayward, from whose original research on the design and plantings of the gardens the author drew liberally.

To Joan Marie Wiecek, whose master's project on the landscape greatly assisted an understanding of and appreciation for Frederick Law Olmsted's effect on Shelburne Farms.

To Kenneth Wheeling, whose book, *Horse-Drawn Vehicles at the Shelburne Museum*, opened up the world of carriages to the author.

And to Richard Janson, whose cultural interpretive workshop explained the architectural roots of the house.

Many other individuals with special knowledge consented to be interviewed. They included Ernest and Ellen St. George, Armande and John Boisvert, Truman Webster, the Reverend J. Linwood Smith, Sr., Emily Wadhams, Sheila Lawrence (interviewed by Marilyn Webb), Sheafe Satterthwaite, Mark Neagley, and Alec and Marshall Webb. For their time, insights and help, the author extends his appreciation.

In addition, he would like to thank Ellen Janson, whose organizational work in the archives eased the formidable job of locating letters, journals, photos and other information.

Photographs came primarily from the archives at Shelburne Farms, with T.E. Marr's outstanding work foremost represented. Marshall Webb also contributed excellent photographs.

Editing and proofreading of the manuscript were done by Peggy Eriksson. Her skills have made the text smoother and better than the author alone ever could have.

And last, but certainly not least, the author expresses his debt to John Lively, editor of *Fine Homebuilding*, for without John's initial interest in the restoration, the seed for this book would never have been planted.

# Illustrations: Credits

Except for photos on pages 41, 65, 82, 86, 88, 89, 90 and 92, all illustrations are from the archives of Shelburne Farms.

Architectural details at the top of each page are adapted from original house blueprints by R.H. Robertson.

# References

Eileen Balderson and Douglas Goodlad, *Backstairs Life in a Country House* (North Pomfret, Vermont: David & Charles, 1982)

Julius Gy. Fabos, Gordon T. Milde, and V. Michael Weinmayr, *Frederick Law Olmsted, Sr., Founder of Landscape Architecture in America* (Amherst: University of Massachusetts Press, 1968)

Charles S. Forbes (ed.), "William Seward Webb" in *The Vermonter*, vol. V, no. 8, March, 1901

Edmund Fuller, *Vermont, A History of the Green Mountain State* (State of Vermont, 1952)

Mark Girouard, *The Victorian Country House* (London: Oxford University Press, 1971)

Susan Cady Hayward, "The Gardens at the Shelburne House" in *The Gardens, A Cultural Interpretive Workshop* (Shelburne Farms videocassette, 1985)

Henry I. Hazelton, "Shelburne Farms" in *New England Magazine*, vol. XXV, no. 3, November, 1901, pp. 267-277

Edwin P. Hoyt, *The Vanderbilts and Their Fortunes* (New York: Doubleday & Company, 1962)

Frank H. Huggett, *Life Below Stairs* (New York: Charles Scribner's Sons, 1977)

Richard Janson, *Architecture, A Cultural Interpretive Workshop* (Shelburne Farms videocassette, 1985)

Del Keppelman, "Shelburne House Gardens," a research project (Shelburne Farms monograph, 1985)

——————————, "Restoration of the Shelburne House Gardens," a research project (Shelburne Farms monograph, 1985)

Alvide Lees-Milne and Rosemary Vevey (eds.), *The Englishman's Garden* (Boston: David R. Godine, 1983)

William C. Lipke, *Shelburne Farms: The History of an Agricultural Estate* (Burlington: University of Vermont, 1979)

Chester H. Liebs (dir.), *The Burlington Book* (Burlington: University of Vermont Historic Preservation Program, 1980)

Virginia McAlester and Lee McAlester, *A Field Guide to American Houses* (New York: Alfred A. Knopf, 1984)

Emily Mead, "Shelburne House Interiors," a manual (Shelburne Farms, 1983)

Roderick Nash (ed.), *The American Environment: Readings in the History of Conservation* (Reading, Massachusetts: Addison-Wesley Publishing Company, 1976)

Robert H. Robertson, "Country House Drawing & Floor Plans" in *American Architect and Building News*, vol. XXI, no. 586, March 19, 1887

Montgomery Schuyler, "The Works of R. H. Robertson" in *Architectural Record*, vol. VI, July 1896-June 1897, pp. 184-218

Vincent J. Scully, Jr., *The Shingle Style* (New Haven: Yale University Press, 1955)

Linda Seavy, "Shelburne House Inn Interior Survey," a monograph (South Hero, Vermont: Circa Interiors, 1984)

Florence Adele Sloan, *Maverick in Mauve, The Diary of a Romantic Age,* with commentary by Louis Auchincloss (Garden City: Doubleday & Company, 1983)

Colonel G. Creighton Webb, *Webbs and Allied Family History, A Genealogy and Biography* (New York: National Americana Society, 1938)

Kenneth E. Wheeling, *Horse-Drawn Vehicles at the Shelburne Museum* (Shelburne, Vermont: The Shelburne Museum, 1974)

Joan Marie Wiecek, "Shelburne Farms: An Historical Study of a 19th Century Agricultural Estate and Plan for the Restoration and Preservation of its Landscape," a master's project (Amherst: University of Massachusetts, 1984)